A Generation Misunderstood:

Generation Next

Author: Bobby Bostic

I dedicate this book to all the lost troubled

kids of the world today,

to the people who do not understand them

and what they go through,

and to the youth searching for meaning,

because it's never too late

to find your way when you are lost.

ISBN: 9780578669540

Book Categories: Juvenile Nonfiction, Social Issues, Adolescence

TABLE OF CONTENTS

Introduction

Imagine how it feels being a child confused and lost in your own home because no one really understands you. For the most part, we grew up as children in a world that we couldn't relate to. The world was moving too fast and most of the adults in our lives were too busy to teach us. The majority of the times we kept our feelings to ourselves because whenever we did decide to express our feelings, we were made to feel stupid for feeling a certain way. Children are very sensitive, but in dealing with their own turmoil, most adults seem to forget this. Also, children are very inquisitive, and they ask a lot of questions as they come of age. They are curious about the world and all its happenings; therefore, they have an endless stream of questions to ask. Sometimes this causes impatient adults much frustration and they snap on kids. It irritates them to be asked so many naïve questions when they have numerous other problems to contemplate about. As a result, there are a great portion of adults who give kids an impatient reply to their questions. Other adults give kids sarcastic responses to their questions and make kids feel stupid for asking. This in turn hurts kids' feelings and discourages them from asking questions. This causes confusion; and confusion amongst children leads to anger. There are a combination of factors that join forces to produce so many angry and confused children. The reasons stated above greatly contribute to this problem.

Children somehow learn to manage and find comfort and understanding in each other. As they get older, they attempt to ignore their state of confusion because no one really wants to be confused in a world that seems to be so sure of itself. Not knowing can be painful because not knowing can hurt you. Yet in their rebellion, most children pretend to be knowledgeable about things and all this does is end up hurting them even more. When you are angry and confused as a child and you have never been properly taught to channel these emotions, this can lead to some children later turning in to violent people. Other children just withdraw deeper into themselves and away from a world that refuses to understand them.

It really hurts a child's feelings when they are made to feel as though they are irrelevant. Kids do things that may seem stupid, but kids ae going to be kids. You have many impatient adults dealing with their own problems and assume that children should know better. They forget that they were once children themselves. Let us look at the big picture. Let us see clearly into some of the issue that have played a major part in the shaping of this generation.

How does it feel to be a child locked inside of a shell because no one really understands you? How does it feel to a child who is loved, but feels like he or she is not loved? How does it feel to be a child who is confused and misunderstood by his or her teachers? How does it feel to be a child who is neglected by the people who are supposed to care for you? How does it feel to be a child whose feelings are constantly hurt by people who do not even realize that they are hurting you? How does it feel to be a child who feels that his or her thoughts and feelings are irrelevant? How does it feel to be a child who grows into adulthood still affected by a scarred childhood? How does it feel to be a child who is full of pain, confusion, and anger that they never really quite get over? How does it feel to be a child who is misunderstood?

We will discuss and answer all of these questions in the up and coming pages and chapters of this book. For the most part it appears like most children of this generation had a normal childhood, but that appearance is very deceiving, especially when you are on the outside looking in. But if you look at the child within yourself or if you remember when you were a child looking out at the world, then you will probably realize that your childhood was not all that normal by ordinary standards. Most adults today still suffer the scars of their childhood and they attempt to block out all of those hurtful experiences that they endured during their childhood. That is the reason why it is so easy for most adults to forget how sensitive they were as children. If they would take this into consideration many adults would not deal with children with the low tolerance level that they do. Such hostility and harsh treatment only add to the pain and anger that so many kids feel today. Then when this pain and anger begin to overflow and the wrath of it is unleashed on society, people begin to wonder what makes these young men and women so angry that they explode the way they do in society today. Only after tragedy upon tragedy has occurred do people in high places begin to hear the underlying cries behind the violent and outrageous actions of these youngsters. Only then do most people seek to find out what motivates these young people to behave so recklessly and lash out the way they do. Only after such countless tragedies do people seek to understand a generation that is so misunderstood. Well in the midst of all these tragedies, we will take a look inside the mind of this generation in order to figure out what makes our youth so violent and disrespectful in this day and   age.

I Am

I am because I am alive

I am because I have suffered and still survive

I am because I see the light

I am because I am one with mankind's plight

I am because I feel

I am because I hurt, and I heal

I am because I exist

I am because I stand up to oppression and resist

I am because I am a human being

One who has felt and seen many a thing

I am because I am here

I am because I love, and I care

I am because I make mistakes

To become better, I am doing whatever it takes

I am because I am not perfect in my doing

Many failures have resulted in the goals that I am pursuing

I am because I keep on trying

I am now, but one day I will be dying

I am because I came and went

I am because when I left the earth, I left my footprint

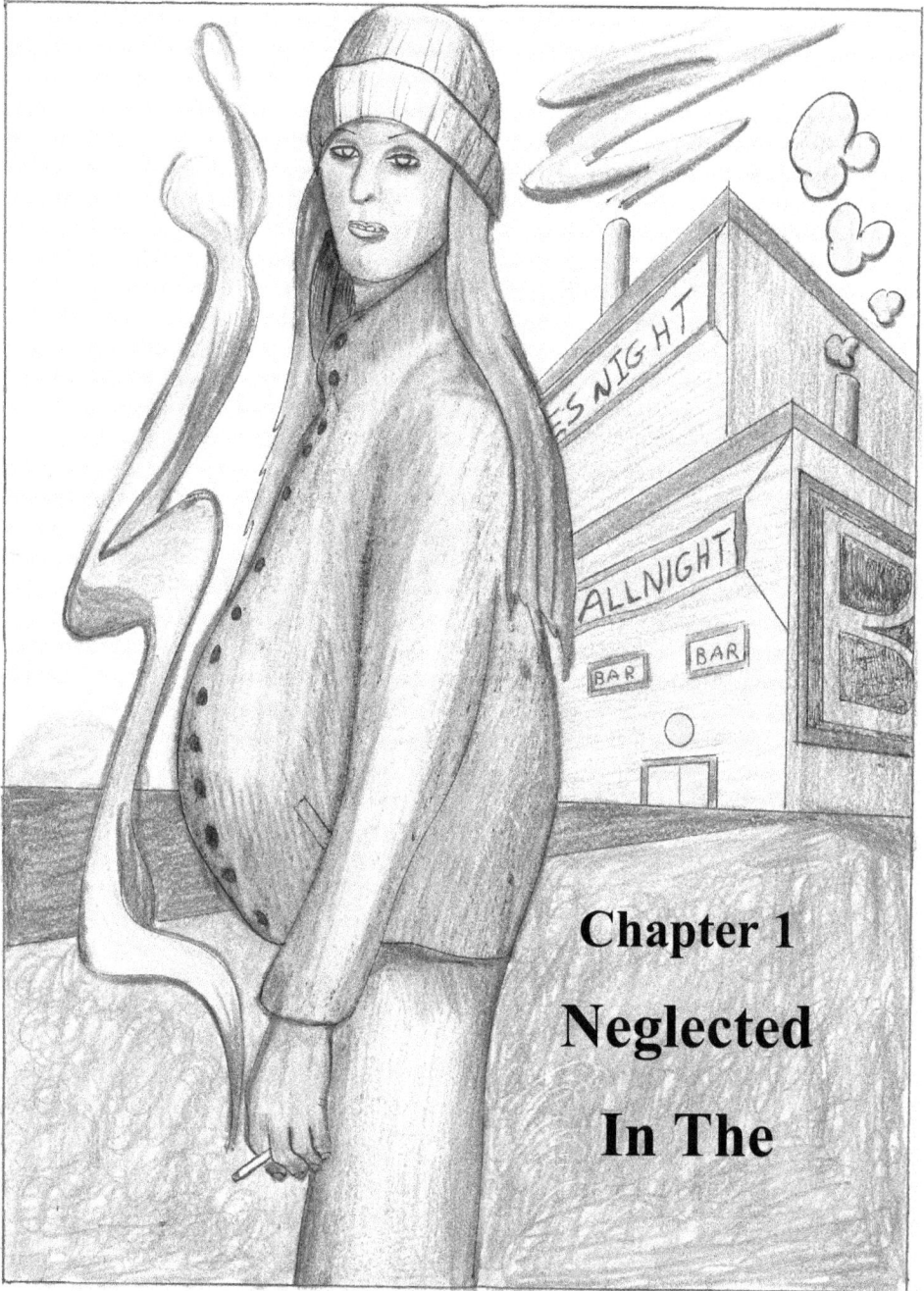

Chapter 1

Neglected

In The

Chapter 1
Neglected in the Womb

One may ask how can a child be neglected in the womb? A child can be neglected in the womb the same way in which it can be neglected at birth and in childhood. For many children today their neglection begins from their very conception. One may ask how can this be? Answered quite simply, it can be done very easily. Many children are born to young unwed mothers. Most of these women who give birth have no idea of what it means to be a mother until their children beget children of their own.

Okay let's take a look at this. We are not pointing the finger. We are only trying to be rational here. Now when a young unwed mother gets pregnant usually that pregnancy was not planned. It is often the result of casual sexual intercourse. In this situation we have a young boy who does not even have an idea of what it means to be a man, less known a father. He can walk away if he chooses to, but the mother cannot. She is forced to deal with this new life that she is carrying around in her stomach. What is she to do? Most young women never plan on getting pregnant. They feel that they have many more years ahead of them in which to start a family. For at this point in their life, they just want to have fun, hang out with their girlfriends, and live life to the fullest.

Oops, uh oh, bam, she's pregnant. Hopefully, she has not been with too many partners so that it will not be a problem to determine who the father of the child is. Usually women detect their pregnancy within two or three months. A young woman who is not expecting and not wanting to have a baby will attempt to deny that she is pregnant for as long as she can. Getting pregnant was the last thing that she wanted.

It is common for young women in the world today to be cigarette smokers, light drinkers, and marijuana users. Women these days like to eat lots of junk foods, fast foods, and sweets. Also, these women like to put perms in their hair. A lot of women continue to engage in these activities throughout their pregnancy. When they are reminded of the harmful effects these actions can have on the birth of their child, these women indirectly ignore these warnings. Having already been restricted enough by virtue of their pregnancy, these women refuse any further infringement upon their freedom. But they never sit down to really consider the amount of damage that these harmful activities can have on their unborn child.

We will briefly talk about some of the adverse effects these sorts of actions have on children. When women smoke during their pregnancy, the nicotine and carbon monoxide inhaled from cigarette smoke enters the mother's bloodstream, crosses the placental barrier, and enters the baby's bloodstream. Nicotine and carbon monoxide cut down the oxygen supply to the baby. It has been noted some studies show that more carbon monoxide ends up in the blood of the unborn baby, than in the blood of the smoking mother. Nicotine also causes narrowing of the blood vessels in the placenta and further reduces the supply of food and oxygen to the baby. Mothers who smoke also face the risk of miscarriage. Marijuana can have the same, as well as, worse effects on an infant. Smoking during pregnancy can cause slower growth and development during the critical time before birth. Such a developmental stunt can last well into the teenage years and perhaps even longer.

Almost everything in a woman's bloodstream passes through to the developing organs of the fetus. Therefore, when a pregnant woman drinks, she exposes her unborn infant to many dangers. Some of the effects are poor circulation, developmental delays, heart defects, mental retardation, and countless other serious complications for the child.

When the mother drinks, the baby drinks also. The alcohol stays in the fetus system longer than it stays in the mother's system. This causes critical prenatal development problems and can lead to fetal alcohol syndrome, which disrupts the infant's nervous system and leads to craniofacial abnormalities. The most adverse effects resulting from drinking while pregnant include withdrawal, fetal alcohol syndrome, and possibly death.

Furthermore, a fetus needs the right nutrients. The baby eats what the mother eats. In today's fast-moving society, many pregnant women eat all kinds of unhealthy food. Most notably is the vast amount of fast food that women consume. Many studies have proven that fast food is detrimental to good health. Many of these foods are not properly processed and are half cooked. What's even worse is the fact that these women do not even properly digest these foods because they are usually in a hurry to do everything, even when it comes to eating.

Everything that enters the mother's body affects the life of the unborn child. If a woman fails to exercise and keep a healthy diet, she is also exposing her fetus to an unhealthy development as a result of her unhealthy lifestyle. The purpose of me stating these medical facts is not to give a full medical overview of the effects of these harmful chemicals on the infant. The purpose in stating these medical facts is to give a brief overview of how mothers neglect their children while they are still in the womb.

Life for an infant actually starts and takes shape before birth. Modern medical technology enables doctors today to better understand the developmental stages of an infant while still in the womb. The most rapid brain growth happens between the fourth month of pregnancy and the sixth month after birth. While still embedded in the womb, internal as well as external events influence the personality of a child. Also, while in the womb, a child has ears and can recognize the mother's voice and touch. When a mother is resentful and vengeful of the child, this message is communicated to the baby before birth.

I have known many women who ignore the warnings of the affects that doing certain things while they are pregnant can have on their fetus. They give such nonchalant replies such as, "my mother constantly drank beer, smoked cigarettes, and did everything else while she was pregnant with me and I was a very healthy and smart baby, so I know that the little things I am doing while I am pregnant are not going to hurt my baby." Little do they realize there are unseen long-term effects that their mother's actions have on them. These things cause serious impairments to babies whether or not they are detected.

Furthermore, it would be a cold act for a mother to continue engaging in these sorts of activities after coming into the knowledge of the damaging effects it may have on her child. Her heart as well as her mother instincts should be enough to influence her not to partake in any risky activities during her pregnancy. Her main concern should be of the baby that she is carrying inside of her womb. Although she did not intentionally try to get pregnant, once she finds out that she is pregnant, any such thoughts should be irrelevant because the reality is that she is now pregnant. Once she knows that she is going to become a mother, she should then put the well being of the fetus above her own needs and wants.

She will have to sacrifice fun, consumption, and other such things in order to protect the short- and long-term health of her unborn child. It is now too late to blame her boyfriend or herself about her pregnancy. Now that she is pregnant, her energies must be focused on safely bringing her baby into this world. She now has to take responsibility even if the child's father is not around to help her.

Many young women are still controlled by their desires to have fun and to continue on living as their friends who are not pregnant. Some women actually try not to let their pregnancy slow them down. In some cases, these women psychologically go on denying their conception until their sixth or seventh month into pregnancy. This affects the child more than anyone. It may not automatically be seen visibly, but these things do affect these unborn infants from the fetal stage, through their childhood, and possibly throughout their lives.

Do these young mothers care? Do they love their unborn child? Yes, they do, but they don't realize the dramatic affects their actions have on their unborn fetus. Why? Because they are too busy concerned with the fun, good times, and good years of their lives. They don't necessarily intentionally do these things, but this still does not change the fact of what their actions are doing to their unborn fetus. The things they are doing hinder the development of some of the baby's brain cells and internal organs.

These young mothers neglect their children in the womb by not eating the proper diets or by not eating adequately enough to provide the fetus with the right amount of nutrients. They neglect these babies in the womb by the improper intake of unhealthy chemicals into their body. Oftentimes, these young women do not engage in any healthy exercises.

Also, some women do not spiritually communicate with the child while in the womb. As a matter of fact, many young women begin verbally abusing the child while it is still in their womb. Instead of accepting their pregnancy and celebrating the future birth of their child, they verbally abuse the baby for being a burden and weighing them down.

An unborn fetus looks to its mother as his or her sole life support system. When a mother fails to provide this subsistence in the womb, a child is neglected in the womb. Neglection in the womb has lasting effects upon a child. A person may ask, how? Well, if a child is neglected in the womb, he or she is not born undamaged and has not been totally nurtured to fully take on its duties in life. A child who has been neglected in the womb is sometimes born seeing the world through distorted eyes clouded by the after-birth effects of the harmful chemicals consumed by his or her mother during her pregnancy.

When a mother fails to get proper prenatal care, she is neglecting her child in the womb. A fetus needs prenatal care to ensure the healthiest pregnancy and birth as possible. This neglection of the child in the womb usually continues until the child is born. After the child is born, a young mother indirectly neglects her child fresh from the womb. This happens when the mother does not give proper, time, love, and attention to the newborn. In some cases, even when the young mother tries to do the right thing, she does not know how to do them properly because she was not given a sufficient amount of love, affection, time, and nourishment when she was a newborn. A baby needs to be hugged and cuddled. A baby needs to be sung to and talked to as well as played with. A young mother can give her child only what she knows how to give. Some young mothers still want to go out with their peers and have fun and work a job, etc. In the process of doing this, her child is desperately missing its mother every hour that she is away. This child needs its mother's time, care, love, and affection. If the child is not provided with these things, then the child is being neglected fresh from the womb. Neglection in and out of the womb seriously batters a child. It leaves an empty cold feeling inside.

As these children grow older, they attempt to compensate for their early neglection by filling the empty spaces in their life. The problem is that these children often try to fulfill the emptiness in their lives in all of the incorrect ways. They seek the love, affection, and attention they were neglected of by means of joining gangs, peer groups, handing in the streets with young troubled frustrated people who can understand and relate to them, as well as by lashing out against society and those whom they feel that they were neglected by. This leads to delinquency, juvenile crime, youth violence, and all the other problems of this troubled generation. So, from a deeper perspective, we can see how neglection in the womb is partially linked to many of the ills that plague generation next. We will further discuss this link and its connection in more detail later on in this book.

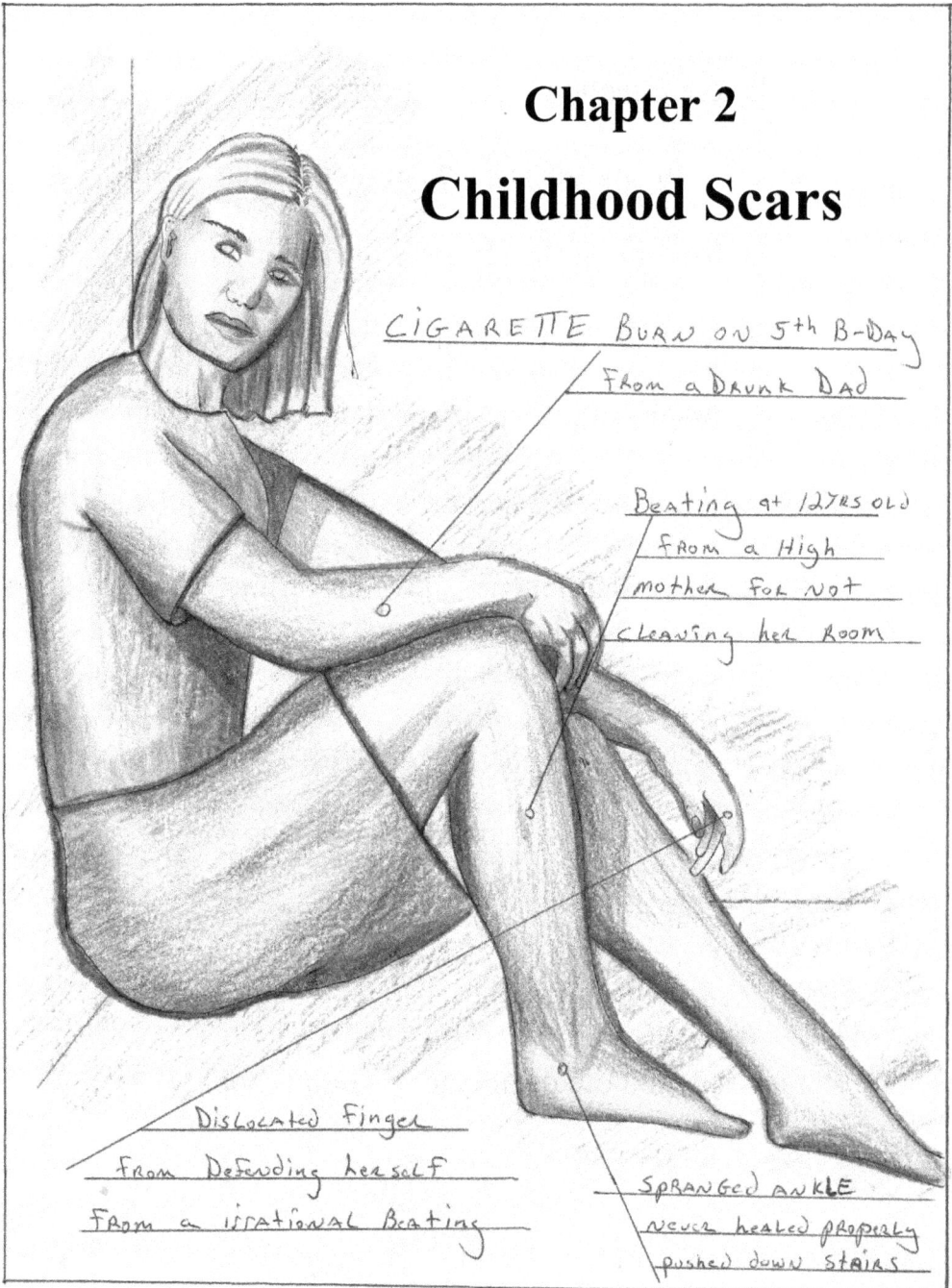

Chapter 2
Childhood Scars

CIGARETTE BURN ON 5th B-DAY
FROM a DRUNK DAD

Beating at 12YRS OLD
FROM a High
mother FoR NOT
CLEANing her ROOM

DisLocated Finger
FROM Defending her selF
FROM a iRRATIONAL Beating

SPRANGED ANKLE
NEVER HEALED PROPERLY
PUSHED DOWN STAIRS

Chapter 2
Childhood Scars

Scars are visible marks that are left imprinted on a person usually after a painful incident. But not all scars are visible. Emotional scars are hidden and sometimes last a lifetime. Those emotional scars from our childhood tend to be the deepest and most lasting of all scars. Most people who carry these scars do not even realize that they are there. These scars are like old wounds that can be reopened by the slightest incident. Where do these scars come from and how did they end up deep within the souls of so many people? Yes, the soul can be scarred too and there is nothing worse than when a child's soul is scarred by his or her loved ones. Here we will discuss how a child can be emotionally and physically scarred and how these scars affect the child's life.

Usually the parents are the first inflictors of these scars. This is the result of a combination of many circumstances. Parents are often frustrated because they have to deal with a slimy boss at work who sometimes treats them like a child. They tolerate the irritating behavior of their boss at work because they need their paycheck in order to pay their bills and keep a roof over their children's head. The other stressful conditions that the parents have to deal with are financial: taxes, insurance bills, mortgage payments; an intolerable landlord, food expenses, transportation needs, and other duties. Having all of these duties can be very stressful and frustrating for an adult. When these adults come home, they are stressed out from a long day. When children get on their last nerves, these adults sometimes take their frustration out on their children.

Physical, verbal, and psychological abuse inflicted upon children causes them to grow into angry violent teenagers who commit crimes at a very young age. Adults use force to crush a child's spirit. On the reverse side of this, physical affection is healthy and plays an important role in the growth and development of a child. However, in today's modern world, sometimes physical contact between mother and child is often very minimal. Rather than affectionately nursing their babies, some mothers give their hungry, attention starved child, a bottle or a pacifier.

There is a process called "bonding" that must happen between parent and child. Many studies have been conducted in this area. Children who receive little or no affection end up with unbalanced emotional health. The majority of physical contact made today between parent and child is in the form of disciplining the child. That is the exact opposite of a much-needed kiss or hug. Children who receive little or no affection do not know how to give affection to their own family or offspring when they get older. Having been taught the wrong concept of affection, people seeking physical comfort turn to sex as a means of affection and warm physical contact.

Children are put into playpens resembling small cages which restrict their movements. Think of the psychological affect that "playpens" have on a child. A child wants affection from his or her mother, but instead is put in a playpen with cold toys and a bottle. So, the child cries out and the frustrated mother screams at the child to be quiet not understanding the child's needs. Babies are not hard to understand. They are only as hard to understand as we make them. Just as this generation is misunderstood, babies are also very misunderstood. Here is a child who is confined to a "playpen" for several hours every day. This child wants to be free to explore its surroundings but is not allowed to because of the physical restraint of the "playpen."

A child is helpless in a "playpen." Here is a child straining to be free, crying out from its soul yearning to be freed from the physical entrapment of this caged designed playpen. This is not a "playpen" to this child, rather it is more like a cage. A baby wants to be free to play. A very intelligent, curious, and inquisitive child cannot do very much in a "playpen." Therefore, we are always seeing babies trying to escape their so-called "playpens" by climbing the bars and kicking at the railing of the "playpens." A child wants to be free, not caged.

Parents incorrectly think that giving a child a thorough beating will teach the child to respect authority figures and be obedient. Numerous psychological studies have proven that this type of treatment produces a frustrated, indifferent, and rebellious child. One psychoanalyst observed that rage from child abuse or child abandonment by parents usually causes the child to develop into a violent dangerous teenager and adult. This is one of the root causes of the violence, anger, and rage that infests this generation.

Often ignored and overlooked by social reformers such as psychologists, social workers, psychiatrists, and childcare workers are the emotional scars that children endure as a result of verbal abuse. Parents verbally abuse their children for different reasons. Some of these reasons stem from good intentions and other parents unconsciously verbally abuse their children for sadistic purposes. Some of these parents have been verbally abused all of their lives by their own parents, siblings, and spouses, and they lash out their discontentment upon their children who are helpless and cannot defend themselves from the verbal onslaught of their parents. Another portion of parents verbally abuse their children because they are frustrated with their situation in life. Then there are those parents who verbally abuse their children with good intentions. They erroneously think that verbally lashing their child will cause enough shame to make the child behave better. What this actually does is produce, in the child, a sense of worthlessness. If the parents who verbally abuse their children take a closer observation, they will see that they themselves still suffer the scars from the callous remarks dished out to them from their parents.

Verbal and physical abuse serve no real purpose in the attempt to correct a child's behavior. It seems as children are seldom rewarded for their good deeds. Children appear to get more attention when they are in trouble. Since children naturally crave and seek attention, they will get in trouble just to get the attention that they do not get when they behave modestly. Adults do not take out the proper amount of time and use the right amount of patience when it comes to dealing with the children of the up and coming generation. Children are afflicted every day with childhood scars. The wounds grow deeper and deeper. We must understand that these scars are not always visible; they are internal emotional wounds. Where is the doctor who heals these wounds? There is no doctor because no one takes the time out to cure this generation. Counselors treat the symptoms, but not the cause. The only doctors we need is our parents. We need them to see and feel these scars and give us the love and affection that only a parent can give.

We need our parents to administer the medicine of care to these deep emotional gashes that protrude our personalities. All we need is our parents' love, care, and affection. It is not too late to save this generation. It is clear that as each new generation is born, child rearing practices become crueler and harsher. Society wonders why we turn out the way that we do? All the pain, hurt, and anger from our childhood is the answer to this question. Further along in this book we will answer this question in more detail. Our childhood scars still hurt us; they never healed, and sometimes the slightest incident can rub our childhood scars raw and bring to surface all of the pain, hurt, and anger these scars caused in our childhood. These childhood scars run deep, and they hurt us right now to this very day.

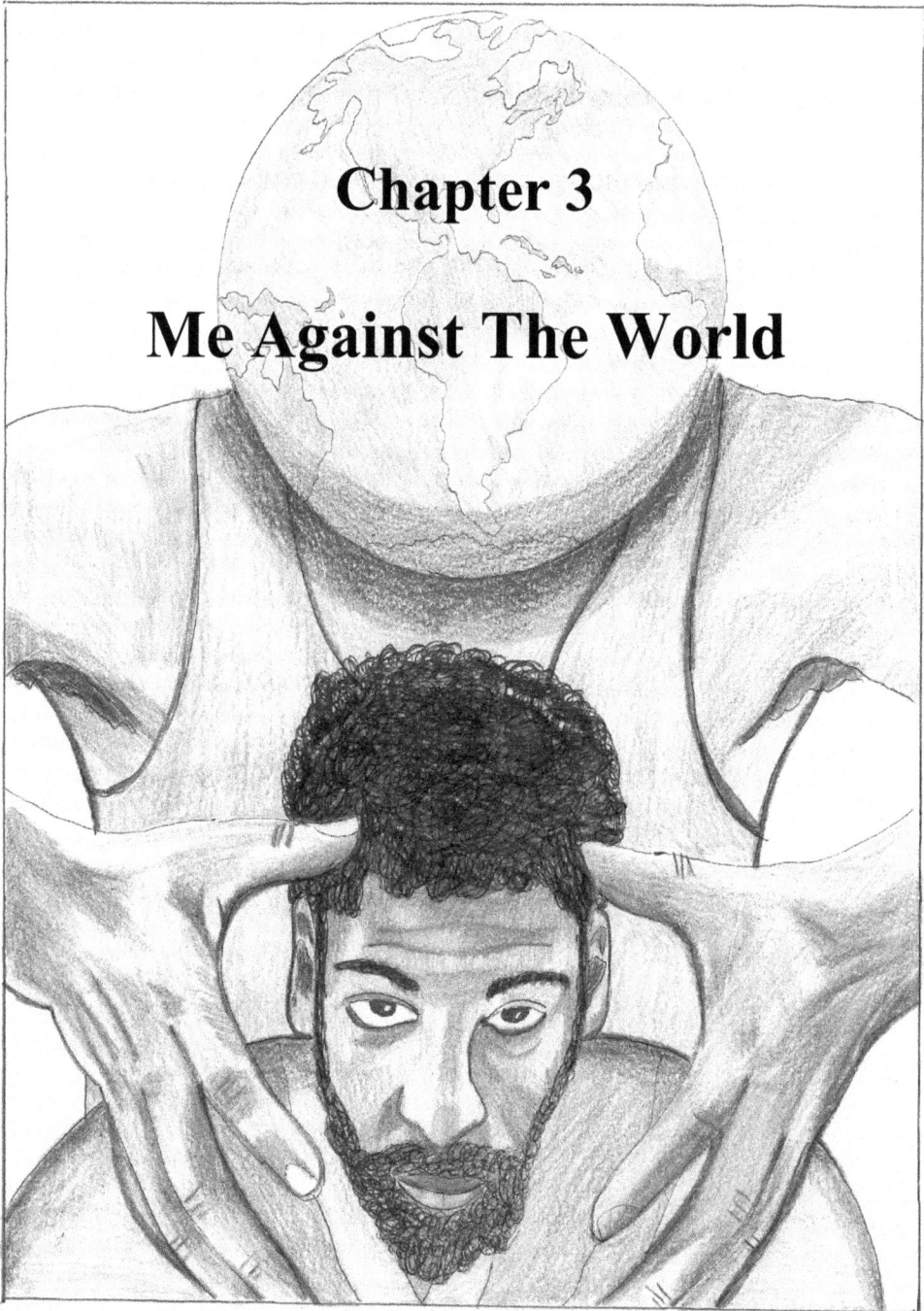

Chapter 3

Me Against The World

Chapter 3
Me Against the World

Every child needs a mothers. They all seek motherly love in one form or another. Sometimes mothers, especially young teenage mothers, are too indulged in everyday fun and fail to give their children the proper amount of love and affection. Henceforth, children do not stop seeking this motherly affection; they will just look for other ways to get this affection. Usually they will seek this motherly affection from a woman who is around them enough. They play an effective role in the growth and development process of children. If it were not for these caring women, our generation would have been much worse than we are today. Imagine a child growing up without a mother. Well, ask around and you will find that various factions of this generation will tell you that even though they grew up with a mother, they still feel as if they did not have one because they feel as if she was not there for them emotionally, mentally, or physically. Many young people feel like their mothers were not really there for them during their childhood. Therefore, they feel like they raised themselves and this is why so many of our youth act like grown ups at such an early age.

Children who seek motherly love outside of home usually do not realize that this is what they are doing until they are old enough to understand.

This void that causes them to seek motherly love causes an enormous amount of pain in children's lives. Adults take advantage of the emptiness in children's lives and this makes it hard for kids to trust people. Later on, kids take on the "I don't care" attitude. When a motherless child goes looking for love in the wrong places, this child often meets with disaster. Some adults avenge their own childhood pain on helpless children as a means to seek comfort. These types of occurrences make the world a painful place to live in. Children do not know how to release their pain and anger, so they keep it inside. What happens to a child when someone takes advantage of their absence of having a mother and uses it for some ulterior motive that the adult wishes to achieve? Just ask the many children of our generation who have been taken advantage of or neglected, and they will tell you the answer to this question. Ask the youth of this faction and they will tell you why they are so frustrated and hurt on the inside. Many of them will not use the above words to describe their internal characteristics, but the actions of their lives tell this story so well.

Looking for love in this world can be a very unpleasant experience. Some adults turn a deaf ear to children's problems. People desire to be there for them, but they can't. Children need to be listened to and paid attention to. When children are neglected of this need of theirs, they tend to feel unloved. Such lack of love at home leads children to seek for love outside of their home. They reach out to anyone who will nurture and care for them. Teachers, people from their community churches, and relatives try to provide children with the love that they are lacking. If they do not understand children, they sometimes do more harm to them than help. Usually, people neglect to tell the child that they love them. They hardly ever give the child hugs and kisses. Usually, they feel that their duty is just to provide for the child financially and physically, and when they do try to do things, they feel like they are invading the child or going beyond their duties. Even when they do reach out to the child in a physical manner, the child feels awkward or either uncomfortable knowing that this caregiver is not their parent. Children begin to feel that the adult is pushing themselves on them or even trying to be someone in their lives who they are not. The child does not intentionally desire to be repulsive or indifferent to someone who is trying to care for them, but they unconsciously resist this love due to the wounds from past experiences from previous caregivers.

If a child feels as though there was no real mother around to raise them, and no one really substituted in the place of their mother, then this type of child usually takes on the "Me Against the World" attitude. This is because of this person feeling alone in this world and unable to trust anyone. Children who were raised in foster homes really tend to feel this way. Children can feel like the whole world betrayed them if no one was there to properly care for them in their childhood. They become so emotionally abused from this lack of love that they attempt to shut off their emotional faculties and try not to feel vulnerable in order to protect themselves from being hurt so much.

It is hard for such kids to trust anyone. There is a wall of protection around them and those people that maybe do want to care for them can understand why this child or adolescent will not let them in. Surely, the kids look at them through suspicious eyes. There have been too many times in which this child opened up willingly only to face more hurt and disappointment when this caretaker could not really be there for them. Even if and when they do open up, it seems as if no one really understands them. Incidents such as these lend reinforcement to children upholding their policy of shutting everyone out and feeling as if it is just them against the world.

Young kids tend to be very sensitive. After having been lied to so many times it is hard to trust anyone. Anytime they do attempt to trust someone, it seems to backfire on them. Simple incidents such as when a possible caretaker fails to keep a promise it can cause the child to develop a distrust for this person. It does not necessarily stop here because some children carry this disposition and outlook throughout their lives. Being unable to overcome these childhood woes, this type of disappointment from one person affects every other relationship that the child enters. When they have been hurt so much, children put up an emotional blockade.

In many aspects, this generation is anti-social, especially so towards older people. The root of this distrust stems from all of the lies that most children were told while growing up. Grown people are used to lies being told in today's society. Lies are just shrugged off or ignored by them, but a child's feelings are terribly hurt when people lie to them. But even when these children grow up, they too begin to look at lies as just a part of life. It is easy for them to recall all of the traditional lies and myth that they were raised on, such as Santa Clause, the Tooth Fairy, Cupid, and other such nonexistent characters. Kids accept these myths as being real, but to find out that these things were false causes children to develop a mistrust of adults.

Generation next also has the "Me Against the World" mentality because they truly feel that the world is against them. Because of stereo typing, they become alienated from the adults in their communities who helped raise them. Many older people shun this generation. It is so bad that some parents disown their children. People do not understand this generation; they do not understand our cultures and they do not understand why this generation readily embraces violence. Therefore, we of this generation are often treated and looked upon as outcasts.

Since the world shuns this generation, this generation also shuns the world. Society rejects the ways of this generation and in turn, this generation rejects the ways of society. Two wrongs do not make a right, but this generation only knows what it has been taught. Most youngsters on the streets will only make a concession towards society when society makes a concession towards them. When you are a person with the "Me Against the World" mentality, you only care for those who you think care for you. Although everyone in the world is not literally against you, in your heart you feel like everyone is against you. The "Me Against the World" mentality is the way that many of our youth think today. Delinquency can easily be traced to this mentality. When a group of youth engage in delinquent acts, they see it as merely having fun. Youth are hostile because being passive allows people to run over you in this world. Adolescents try to stay far away as possible from this because they already feel that adults have been running over them all of their lives. Engaging in delinquent acts and violent behavior is the adolescent's way of striking back.

Today's youth are also very insensitive because being sensitive during their childhood has caused them much of the pain that they feel inside. These adolescents were taught at a young age that for them to embrace their sensitivity would be a grave mistake. Kids tend to close up within themselves and block the world out and this is the beginning of them taking on the "Me Against the World" attitude.

For the most part, this is also a fearless generation. Fearless because many youths feel as though they have nothing to lose. They see the world falling apart right before their eyes. They witness the futile wars that are ongoing around the world. Many youths see death outside of their door. They witness their peers dying every day. They see and hear of the atrocities that are being inflicted upon innocent people every day. Youth do not really trust older people. Older people are looked upon as the representatives of the establishment, and the establishment is seen as hypocritical. Today's youth are rebelling against the establishment and all its played-out traditions. The "Me Against the World" mentality makes it easy for a person to defy the rules of society. When you feel that the world is against you, you defend yourself by being against the world. This is how this generation feels at the core of its heart.

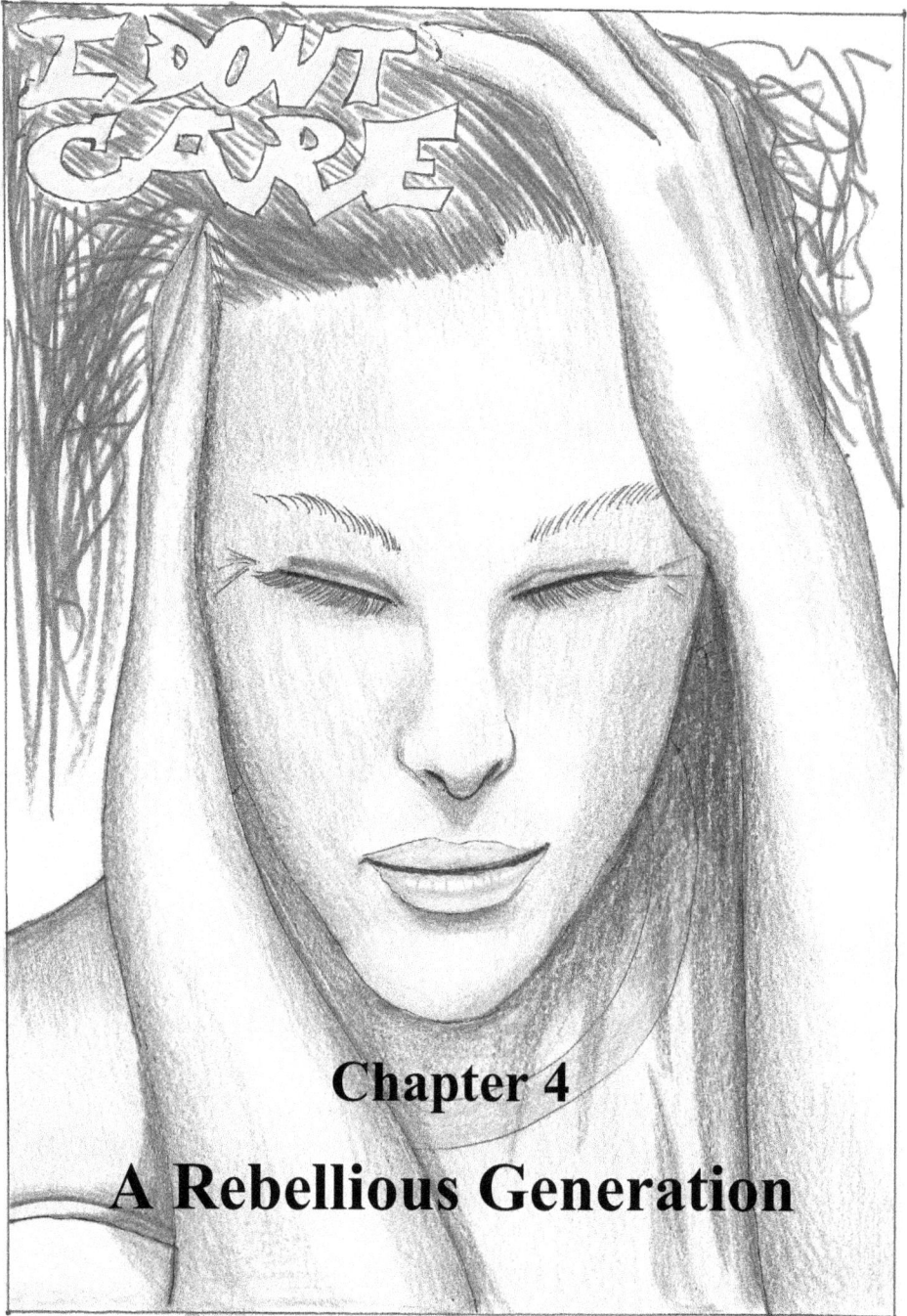

I DON'T CARE

Chapter 4

A Rebellious Generation

Chapter 4
A Rebellious Generation

Rebellion is a common response to rejection. Most of this generation in one way or another felt rejected as kids. Some of us felt this way because we thought that no one really loved us even when we knew better. More often, this was not the case. Many people around us, loved us. They just did not know how to show us love because they had not been shown how to love in the proper manner. As kids we were very sensitive to this. Most adults paid this no attention. They were insensitive to our fragile feelings in the same way in which their parents were insensitive to them. This is the result of a type of continuous cycle that I spoke of earlier in this book. The rejection that this generation felt as kids lead us to act out the rebellion that we still display to this very day.

Often the root of this rebellion is the rejection that we felt as children. All kids go through stages of rejection among their peers. Some kids handle this more sensitive than others and the results can be drastic. We see some adults calling each other "big babies" and "crybabies" because of how they respond to disappointments and let downs. In particular, these adults respond like this because they have never been healed from the rejection they felt as kids. Usually these types of adults are rebellious in one form or another.

Many of them go through life feeling rejected because they have never been healed from their childhood scars. Children do not come out of the womb rebellious. From constant exposure to rejection, rebellion then becomes a dominate trait of some children. Here we have a clear picture defining one facet of this generation's rebellious nature.

Rebellious people are considered to be angry people. Look at this generation and you can clearly see our anger written upon our faces. Even when most of us smile on the outside, we are still angry inside. We are angry because we feel that the world has treated us bad since our birth. I do not speak for everyone of my generation, but I do speak for a vast majority of us. All of us may not put the words this way, but if a reasonable observer were to look closely and listen to this generation, that person will be able to hear these words I am saying in our actions, in our conversations, and most notably in the music we listen to.

This world makes this generation feel as though we are a burden to the world. When this world gets tired of this generation being a burden on it, we sense this and therefore we rebel against this world. This generation never meant to be a burden to this world, so how can we be blamed for being called into existence. It is not our fault that we were born into this world of poverty and confusion. It hurts so much to see that this world considers us as a burden. At the same time this world claims to love us. The actions of those people who claim to love us says something different from their words. We feel the active hostility from the veterans of the world. The people that should be guiding us are the ones that lead us astray. That is why we rebel against this hypocritical world. I am not saying that the sentiments and the actions of this generation are justified per se. No, I am not saying that, but what I am putting forth are the reasons why this generation is so misunderstood, and why we are the way that we are today. My point in digging to the root of our actions is to show that this generation in its actions are only blindly protesting against this hypocritical world. We protest in an immature way because in our rage, we only desire to unleash our anger and disappointment at the world. All other strategies of protest have failed our parents and their parents before them so therefore we are only a carbon copy of all the anger and rebellion that our parents, grandparents and great grandparents felt before us. They may have been able to restrain themselves, but the anger that pumps through the artery vein of this generation is too great to suppress.

Oh yes, they call us a generation of unrest, but I maintain to you that we are only a generation of protest. We protest by means of venting our anger letting this world know that we are not a standby generation. Because of our radical culture and lifestyle the world has treated this generation like a stranger so it should not surprise the world when we lash out making it known that we want the attention, love, and affection that we never got as children.

The elders of this world tell this generation that violence is not the answer to our problems. They point out that most of our problems stem from our rebellious actions. Psychologists and psychiatrists try to figure us out, but in truth their diagnoses are full of error. They can only speculate what this generation is about. Ever since our birth no one really listened to us or paid us any attention, therefore we felt rejected and our response to this world's rejection of us is to rebel against the world. And you see the youth of the world rebelling very hard today.

A Closed in Generation

My generation feels closed in. The authorities have come to the conclusion that they must contain and control this generation. They have implemented many rules, policies, statutes, ordinances, and laws by which to accomplish this. Unbeknownst to them is that all of the rules and regulations only makes us even angrier and rebellious. We are aware that the world has closed us in. We only desire to be a part of this world.

Why does this generation protest so violently? This generation feels that violence is the only way that this world will feel us. Why have we come to this conclusion? When we protest peacefully it appears the world continues to ignore and reject us. Sick and tired of this, we begin to rebel visibly and radically. If you ask the average teenager why do we behave so violently, they will confirm my position. This generation is so violent because this generation is very angry inside.

We feel closed in, so we rebel to escape. Deep inside we only want to interact with the world. When we try to react peacefully with the world, we are still rejected. This causes the scars from our childhood to reopen and we violently protest against the world. Most angry youth unconsciously think that violence is the only way this world hears our voice. We feel so closed in and trapped. We try to get the world to understand, but we still end up so misunderstood. By being misunderstood, we again feel rejected. Misunderstanding also leads to confusion and of course confusion leads to chaos. Yes indeed, we are a chaotic generation. There are many negative

labels this generation is labeled by, but at the root

of it all, we are just very misunderstood.

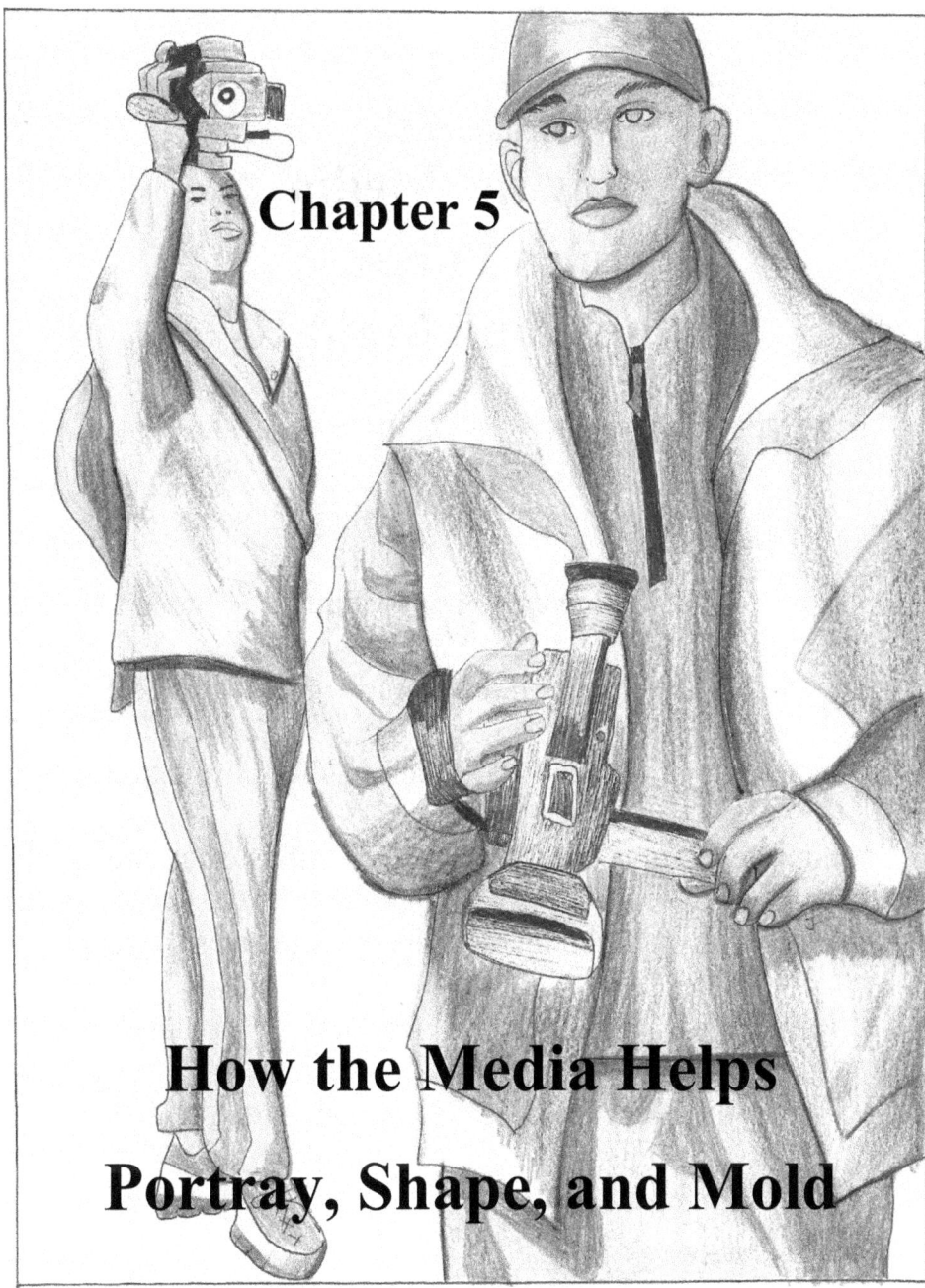

Chapter 5

How the Media Helps
Portray, Shape, and Mold

Chapter 5
How the Media Helps Portray, Shape, and Mold Us

The media mentally controls this generation through subliminal seduction. It influences our values; it creates manipulating images in our minds, and it helps set the trends of our culture. Much of the information this generation knows are the things that we learned through the media. The media consists of a variety of outlets that are used for mass communications such as: television, radio, video, games, magazines, computers, the internet, and newspapers. Overall, the media is a money-making profit system that sells any and everything ranging from sex to soda. In the process of all of this unrestricted selling, the media is also responsible for selling our children a culture of violence as if it were the best purchase that they could make in life. Children are very easily influenced and are open to suggestion. Their minds are like pottery waiting to be shaped by the society in which they live and the things they see and hear around them.

Our children's favorite role models are those whom they see on the television screen. Almost every child has aspired to be a movie star one day. At least in their early years they emulated one or more of these stars in their everyday life. Movies come out that cater to youth's taste and sets the dress codes and becomes a trend setter among adolescents for half a year or so until the next hippest movie comes out and does the same thing. Children at their earlier ages are exposed to a constant appetite of violence by watching cartoons. Some people wonder what harm can there be in watching cartoons? They must understand that the message sent by cartoons is subliminal. Almost all cartoons contain some amount of violence. Even the most innocent cartoons sometimes send out the wrong message. In cartoons you see a lot of destruction. You witness things being blown up, people being shot and dying, cars exploding, guns being fired, and all the wrong things that stimulate a child and have an influence on their thinking. As children grow older, they begin to watch a more constant stream of violent television programs.

Now let's discuss the various forms of media and talk about how they play a role in influencing and helping to shape the violent materialistic nature of today's generation. First, we will talk about the most notorious aspect of the media that helps to corrupt the minds of our children. The average child spends more time watching television than they spend with their parents. With all the many different fields of entertainment and mind-boggling shows, who is in effect raising today's children: their parents or the television?

We Were Raised By The T.V.

Consensus show that the average child watches at least four hours of television every day. On weekends, they may watch anywhere from 6 to

8 hours of television. By the time a child reaches the age of 18, it is estimated that he or she will have viewed about 200,000 or more acts of violence on television. Most of the present generation and the up and coming generation are being raised by the television. The biggest influence in their life is the T.V. Their role models and superheroes are movie stars and actors. Most of all the sports on television are replete with violence and unrestrained aggression such as hockey and boxing. Kids show more interest in television programs than they show in school. Why? Because what is being shown on television is exciting and full of action while school is boring. Some kids sit in school and daydream

about their favorite television shows and cannot wait to get home to watch them.

If a child spends more time watching television than the child spends with its parents, it is logical to assume that the T.V. is the biggest influence in the child's life. Parents teach discipline, but television teaches a different lesson, and it is too often the wrong lesson. There are no real restrictions on the television. People do what they want to do on television and their anger is usually expressed through violence. How are kids supposed to channel and release their anger? Well, television gives them a good idea on how to do so. Kids begin to fantasize about violence and they directly and indirectly experience it in their everyday lives.

There are many infamous television sitcoms that are said to have a very negative effect on children. Most of these shows are aimed at and cater to a youthful audience. Some people fail to see a direct link between these television shows and the violence that is carried out by so many young people today. There is definitely a connection between the two.

A lot of the things that kids know today are things that they learned from the television. So, we ask ourselves, who is the true teacher of our children? Why is it that kids disregard what they learn at school, but apply what they learn from television to their real lives? For one, the world of television appears to be so real and the world of school seems to be based on the past and irrelevant to what is going on today. The schoolteachers seem so minute compared to the larger than life movie stars. Schoolteachers tell kids about their reality while television sells them drama.

The Different Dimensions of Television

Television has many different dimensions. Each one of these dimensions has a certain amount of influence on the minds of our children. The most compelling of these dimensions that grasp the attention and desire of most kids today is that of vanity, violence, glamour, glitter, fame, sex, and killing. The majority of television shows do not have a moral context. Their only purpose is to entertain, and they cater to the lower desires of people. The positive concepts that are shown on television are seldom watched and usually have very low ratings. Television sells sex and most kids have unrestricted access to T.V. Many negative aspects of life are constantly flashed before the eyes of children tempting them to think about sex at much earlier ages than the children did in past generations.

One of the most outlandish aspects of television is its depiction of glory and luxury. Two decades ago, the good guys were always the stars of the show, but now the bad boys are seizing the spotlight on the big screen. These degenerating characters are whom our children are beginning to look upon as role models. Why? These characters are free, and they have no rules to follow. Also, these characters are rebellious, and they defy anyone who attempts to put any restraints on their freedom. Most kids wish that they could live like this and they dream of the day when they get older and will be able to do it. The images on the screen tell a story, and the message subliminally sent to our children is all too often a negative message. The orientation towards sex and violence starts somewhere and for most kids, this orientation begins right in the comfort of their home via the television screen.

Television has the power of such that it invades the mind and triggers the emotional stimulus totally subduing its audience. Watching television can become an addiction that most people do not even realize they have. Television offers people (children in particular) an escape from the reality of the world in which they live.

Although much of television is fake and scripted, it appears to be very real to our children. Visual images on the screen penetrates the psyche of children.

Some movies and television shows attempt to downplay violence and show its negative consequences, but the scenes of violence throughout the program intrigues children and earns their admiration. Such entertainment venues as comedy teach our children all of the wrong aspects of fun. Most comedians are disrespectful and do not care whose feelings they may hurt with their jokes. Comedians often mock politicians, sending the message to children that politicians are funny men and not really due the respect that they are given. Some people put other people down through jokes so that they may feel better about themselves. Kids follow this example without the least amount of hesitation. So many kids hurt each other's feelings through the telling of jokes that this problem goes unchecked. The entertainment industry classifies comedy as a medium of entertainment that is harmless to everyone. But this same harmless mocking that goes on among adolescents sometimes turns deadly when our youth go over the edge and explode in a rage of violent acts because they were hurt by the mocking that has been directed towards them for so many years.

Many of the ills of the world in society are played down and overlooked. Television is definitely one of the ills of society that is not seen as such by those who are in control of the media. It does not go unnoticed by common everyday people, but it does go unchecked. And as long as it remains unchecked it will remain as a major problem in our society. A steady diet of television only corrupts the morals of children and orientates them towards a violent outlook on life.

Youth and Music

It is a widely known fact of the problem that music presents for today's youth. At the same time, music can be seen as positive because it is a creative outlet for youth to express their views. Youth prove the superiority and complexity of their minds by hearing a song once and memorizing the song's verses. Since music in general can be viewed as being positive, why do so many adults and politicians lobby against certain brands of music? Most notorious on their list is heavy metal music, hard rock, rap music, and hypnotic music. The lyrics of these kinds of music are often hardcore and explicit. Most of this music promotes sex, drugs, guns, violence, murder, and other sorts of negativity. Much of the lyrics are vulgar and derogatory. Women are constantly degraded and defiled in the songs. It is well known that music heavily influences the youth of today's generation.

Music has a very hypnotic effect and it stimulates a person's senses. It can invade the human mind almost to the same extent that television does. Youth listen to their music at a super loud volume. Without going off into much detail, it is clear that much of the music that is made today has a negative influence on our children and corrupts their minds. The music industry is another media outlet that helps to shape our adolescents' culture of violence, crime, and rebellion that is so prevalent among the younger generation.

Kids and Violent Video Games

The violence in video games present a crucial link between children and the violence that they so readily engage in. Refuters of this theory contend that video games are harmless. Well, let's talk about this. Video games used to be innocent and clean fun. Now, they have become more realistic with aminated life like figures. Most of these games are based on the opponents killing each other and dismembering each other's body. In more than 75% of these games, buildings and cars are being blown up. Kids get a very high adrenaline rush while playing and imitating the video characters while using very aggressive language. Children have been known to play these games for a period of up to five hours a day.

What harm is there in an innocent game? Games have a lasting psychological effect. These games are 65% pure killing. Blood splatters all over the screen and there is constant noise and real-life screams of people who are inflicted with pain. Virtually all through the game, there is killing and destruction. There is no moral significance whatsoever in these games. When kids are constantly killing their opponents on these games without any consequences and legal repercussions, it tends to have a certain effect. The effects vary depending on the temperament and experiences of the child. It is true that violent video games are not a threat to all children. Many positive kids, as well as adults of great achievement, play violent video games for the purposes of fun and recreation. But what about those kids who already feel hopeless and on the edge? What about those kids who feel left out and ignored in life? What about those children who may feel suicidal? What about those kids that are given no attention and feel as if no one really cares for them? As for the more unfortunate children, these violent video games help to psychologically train and prepare them for the mindset and emotional tolerance they need to carry out their real life violent actions on their peers, schoolmates, listless adults, and a world that they feel has tortured, teased, and taunted them for so many years.

Thus far we have established how outside sources can be faulted for the desperate position that adolescents are in when they carry out violent and often fatal acts on each other and those who are around them. The violence in video games can be associated with these violent outrages. The constant killings that go on in these games helps to diminish a child's sense of moral inhibition. When these children are filled with seething anger and constant rejection and feel like killing someone, these games help to serve as a psychological trainer for children to engage in such violent acts.

Magazines

Magazines definitely present a problem among youth. A lot of magazines are full of filth and useless propaganda. The majority of magazines advocate and sell sex. Magazines are read more than anything else by youth. They read all kinds of magazines. Their favorite magazines are those that cover music, cars, fashion, and sex. Most kids have unlimited access to these magazines. Most of the explicit magazines target a youth audience. Kids are exposed to guns in magazines also. They borrow their extravagant style of dress from the fashion pages of these magazines. Children read about the luxurious lifestyles of their favorite music stars through magazines. Little boys can look at naked women and conjure up all kinds of fantasies in their minds. These magazines are everywhere and are not difficult for children to get.

Kids are not monitored when they read magazines. They are influenced by whatever may catch their interest no matter how explicit it may be. The comic sections of these magazines are very ridiculous and pointless. Children are exposed to all types of nonsense and garbage in these magazines that they are reading. Half-naked women even advertise such simple things as gum. These magazines sell sex and are replete with entertainment aimed at our children. Without going into further detail, we can clearly see how many of the magazines that are on the market today.

The Internet

The internet is a very all accessible outlet of the media. A child can locate almost anything on the internet ranging from porn to their favorite song. They can even watch movies and go shopping on the internet. Even more the internet has such commodities as chat rooms and e-mail. A chat room is an online communication medium by which people from all over the world can talk to each other. The problem that this poses for children today is that when they're on these chat lines, kids can meet some dangerous and unsafe people. Many tragedies and fatalities have taken place because kids have met someone online and then took further steps of meeting that person face to face without any supervision whatsoever.

On the internet, kids have access to X-rated porn. Unsupervised and unmonitored, kids have access to almost anything on the internet. Most explicit and X-rated websites require that their subscribers be at least 21 years of age. This does little or nothing to discourage children from logging on to these sites. With unlimited access to almost anything in the world, via computer screen, the internet definitely plays a major part in shaping the morals and values of this generation.

A Review of The Media and Generation Next

The media is a manipulative system of psychological control powered by the most sophisticated technology, which flamboyantly displays sex, drugs, murders, wealth, fornication, violence, and crime. Children spend a lot of their time being entertained by the media. The problem is not the media itself, but the things that are broadcast through the media. These things are corrupting the minds of our children at a very young age. The theatrics shown on the television screen are very hypnotic and mind controlling. Such powerful theatrics bare heavy on the psyche of children and begin to have a strong influence on how kids think. Seeing things through the eyes of the media is a far cry from seeing things through the eyes of reality.

There is a term called "media brainwashing." A simple definition of this term is that the media brainwashes people, namely its audience, especially children. Brainwashing is when someone or something deceptively imposes their ideas on someone and makes them theirs. The media is well known for doing this and many brainwashed people (i.e., children) look at the world through the eyes of television.

The media excites, intrigues, and captivates its audience. It holds their undivided attention. People become emotional, excited, and subliminally seduced by the media. Movie stars and musical artist produce a constant flow of filth, nudity, unwed sex, drugs, over all immoral activities.

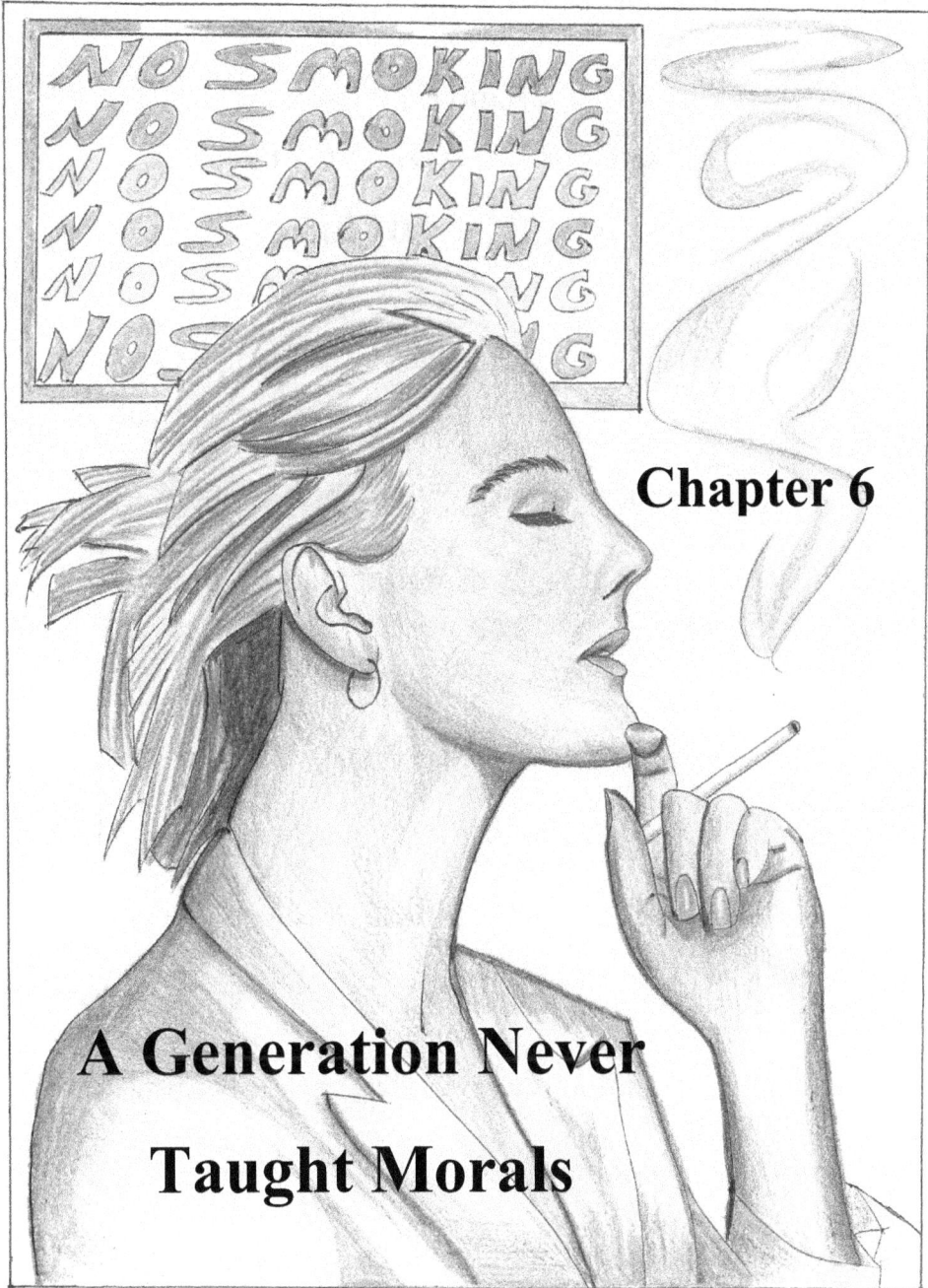

Chapter 6

A Generation Never

Taught Morals

Chapter 6
A Generation Never Taught Morals

Generation next is a generation that was never taught morals. Our parents and elders will say that this is not true. Well okay, to a certain degree they have a point. The majority of morals that were taught to us was contradicted by the so-called teachers of those morals. Older people so often preach to younger people about the principles of living a moralistic life, but they contradict their own teachings by engaging in immoral actions. The concepts of this world have become so corrupt in every realm that even the religious circles seem to accept the immoral actions of its adherents due to the so-called human weakness. The best place for a person to learn morals is in a religious institution. The problem in today's society is that many immoral practices go on right within these religious institutions. The actions of these hypocritical teachers are in opposition to the messages they teach. It seems like they have become so acquainted with being hypocrites that this has become an acceptable practice to them. Now how does this affect those coming up under the guidance of these types of people?

Another aspect of the reasons why this generation has never been taught morals is because we never learned morals at home. Many of tomorrow's children are being born under the parentship of a single mother. The problem with this is that most of them are still very young and wild in their ways. We were raised watching all kinds of immoral things on television, and this is all we see around us. Being immoral is the normal practice of the world today. Even those so-called decent family members and friends who took us to houses of worship practically lived immoral lives, and the morals they instilled in us soon wore down and became tainted by the world.

People may wonder what we mean when we say, "a generation never taught morals?" It is a generation who were raised up watching filthy television, playing violent video games, surfing the internet, and very rarely going to church or any other religious institution. Such a generation quickly begins to see immorality as a normal way of life. That is why kids are so quick to engage in so many immoral practices and have no moral qualms about it whatsoever. Many conservative adults consider such things as tongue piercings as being immoral. Youth just consider it as a part of their culture. Adults wonder why youth have to go so far as to put holes in their bodies to express themselves. Kids see no harm in it, and they are proud of their unique style of dressing. Some parents are taken aback at what they consider their children's outrageous dress codes. The question still remains: are these actions immoral?

Well let's have a further discussion on this subject. There is an endless list of things that conservative people consider to be immoral about this generation. For instance, many young people are wearing tattoos. Tattoos are considered to be immoral for a number of reasons. First there is the medical dangers associated with tattoos such as the risk of catching AIDS, skin infections, and other contagious diseases. Second, there are the moral principles of not defiling the sacred human body. Third, it is considered useless and disrespectful for so many youths to be wearing tattoos that represent stupid things and pointless symbols. Tattoos of human skulls, the grim reaper, gang signs, dogs, and other anonymous symbols seem to serve no useful purpose. Still, an increasing number of youth flock ahead of each other to get these tattoos. A portion of them get their whole arms or back covered with tattoos. Others even tattoo their faces and foreheads.

What do their parents say about these actions? Just like everyone else, they are at a loss over this issue. Their kids usually do these things without their permission or consent. But surprisingly, there are a large percentage of parents who feel helpless and allow their kids to do a lot of these things.

Other parents just shrug when their kids do these things because they consider such fashion statements by their children as part of the culture of their kid's generation. Who teaches the kids this stuff? Most youth get it from their peers, but where do their peers get these styles of dress from? Is it the media? Or their favorite celebrities? Weren't these kids taught better? Did not their parents teach them better morals and values than they are displaying?

Yes, the children of this generation were taught certain things growing up. But this generation was taught that a lot of immoral things were wrong because what was once considered immoral in the past is now accepted as normal today. A prime example of this is how a great number of young women wear skimpy clothes and flaunt their body parts. Even in elementary schools you will see very young girls wearing tight clothing and acting very provocative. In shopping malls, you can even see baby clothes being sold that resemble the skimpy clothing styles of older women. There are some designer shorts called daisy dukes that come well above the thigh. Young girls as young as seven years old can be seen wearing these shorts. It is very immoral for young women to be exposing their buttocks and other body parts. Even when these women cover themselves up, they still wear tight fitting clothing designed to show off their shape.

Is it immoral for young men and women to wear baggy jeans? Is it immoral for children to wear pants that hang below their buttocks? The slang term for this is called "sagging." Of course, adults do not understand these fashion trends. Most adults see no logic in such ludicrous dressing styles. Their position on clothing is that they were made to fit and cover up a person's body. But the average teenager sees nothing wrong with wearing baggy pants.

Looking at the bigger picture, we must come to the conclusion that if this generation was ever taught morals it must have forgotten them. Also considering the things that have been said, it seems that for the most part, this generation was raised around immorality and became immoral by way of growing up in an immoral world. One more question still remains unanswered. Okay, even if these children were raised in an immoral world, did their parents teach them the proper morals and values? Yes, many parents taught their kids better. The thing is that the overall society does not teach kids to be moral. Society makes immorality acceptable and even desirable. Can we blame society for the immorality of adolescents today? In part, yes we can.

What about slang language? Is it immoral for youth to twist the original language and make up hip slang words? This is not considered too much of a problem within itself. The problem comes in when so much vulgarity enters the slang language. Kids use vulgar words a lot these days. They hear so much cursing going on around them and they are constantly exposed to such foul language through the media. Recording artists curse throughout their most popular songs. Movies, television sitcoms, and cartoons use foul language throughout the scripts. How does this affect the precious developing minds of our children?

Constant exposure to such negativity through the media and the environment in which they live in sends our children the message that immortality is just the normal way of life. Many kids do not have a true concept of God and religion, so they live their lives according to the rules of society. In society, they learn firsthand about the freedom of speech and the freedom of expression. The trouble with this is that it can get very vulgar and immoral. Even those children that were raised in the church saw the corruption around them. It seemed like almost everyone and everything around them was immoral to some degree. And when they were away from home around their peers, most of which were not raised in the church, peer pressure combined along with their peer culture quickly eroded any morals they may have known before.

Does This Generation Have a Conscience

Older people sometimes sit back and look at the violence and madness of this generation and honestly question whether or not this generation has a conscience. They occasionally wonder if these youngsters care. Do they care whom they hurt? They see most young people as careless, reckless, lacking morals, and devoid of a decent conscience. Older and elderly people no longer blame these young people's parents because some of these older people helped raise the children of this generation. But still they wonder where us kids went wrong and why we are so cold inside? The violent actions of this generation do make it seem as if we are a generation without a conscience.

This generation does have a conscience. I know that our actions say otherwise. We kill one another, we slander each other, we are often disrespectful, and overall, we have an "I don't care" attitude. But this goes back to our lack of morals. Because this is where it begins. Morals and the conscience are close associates. Without strong moral principles, the conscience tends to fade into the shadows. A strong moral nature strengthens the conscience. It would seem that an immoral generation would be a generation that does not have a conscience. I proclaim to you that this generation does have a conscience. The conscience of this generation has been dimmed because of our growing up around so much immorality. Furthermore, this generation is full of a lot of anger and our conscience has to be played down to a certain degree in order for us to defy the norms of society and unleash our anger.

The conscience is defined as a person's awareness of right and wrong with regard to his or her actions. A person with morals is defined as a person who is concerned with the principles of right and wrong behavior. As stated earlier, this generation lacks morals. Behavior that they were told was wrong in religious settings seemed okay in society. Does this generation know the difference between right and wrong? Much of what seems wrong to older people is considered to be okay to young people. Why is this? Young people growing up today are raised much different from the way people were raised in past generations. The things that were looked upon as wrong back then, are looked upon as the cool thing to do today. This generation does know the difference between right and wrong. There is a distinction because the standards of right and wrong are measured different by this generation than how it is measured by conservative people. Our way of life is different from other people. Having said this much about this topic, I think that it is logical to conclude that in some ways, this is a generation that was never properly taught morals.

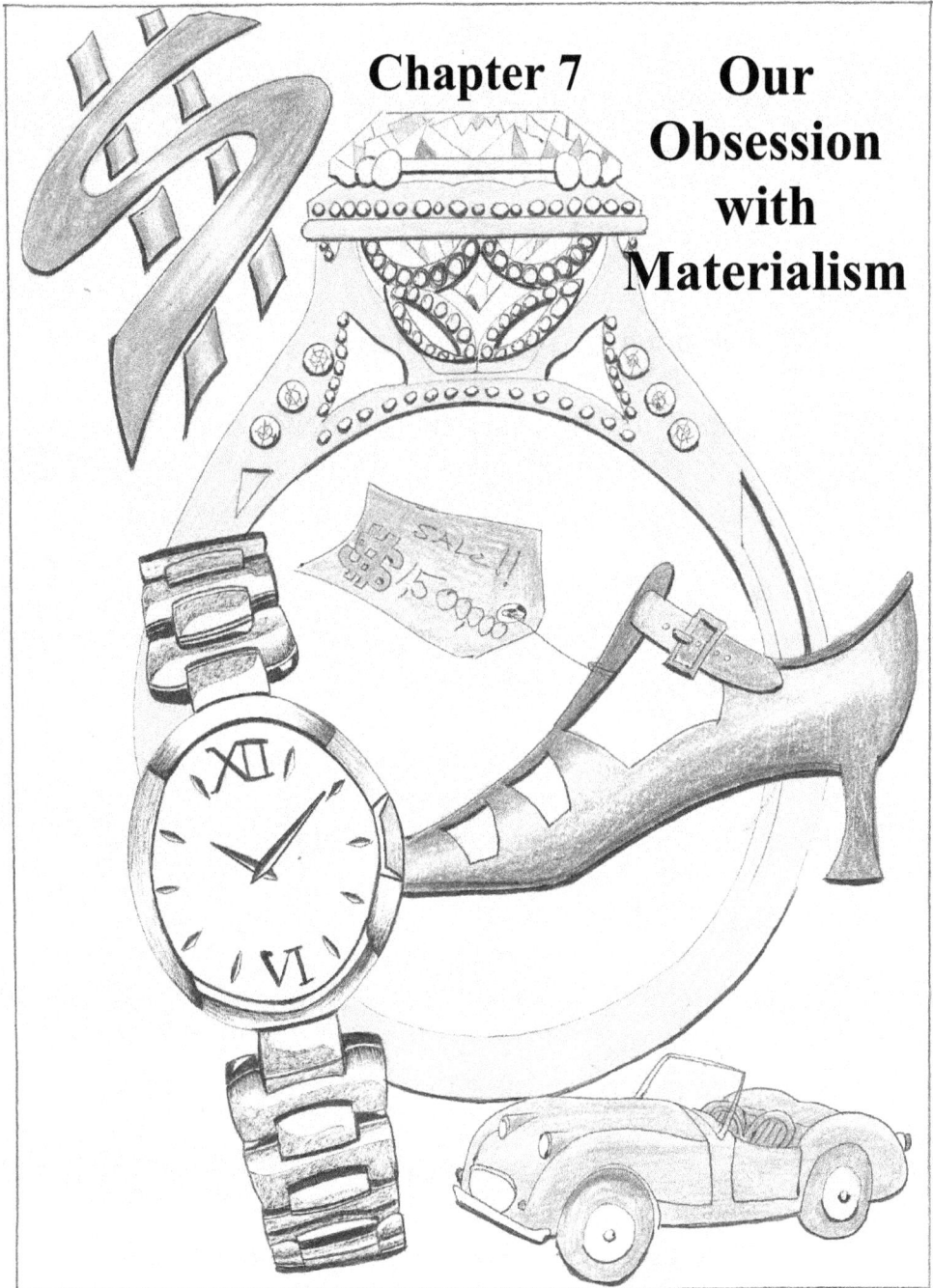

Chapter 7

Our Obsession with Materialism

Chapter 7
Our Obsession with Materialism

It is often said that the present generation is one of the most materialistic generations that the human family has ever known. The distinction with former materialistic generations and the present generation is that the people of the past worked hard for the material benefits that they reaped. This generation is obsessed with materialism. It is a major part of our culture. Of course, there is nothing wrong with wanting to have nice material possessions. The problem starts when you acquire hoards of material things for all of the wrong reasons. If you ask the average young person why do they want to have nice things, they will say that they want nice things because they like them, and it makes them feel better about themselves. Furthermore, having the best things makes them feel like they are someone important. If you are unfortunate and unable to afford the finest things, you are labeled as a nobody. Being a nobody means that you will become subject to mocking, teasing, jokes, and harassment from your peers.

A child does not want to be subject to the jokes and taunts of his/her peers because the child is unable to afford nice material possessions. All we see through the media and advertisements is the promotion of nice material possessions. This is an impatient generation, therefore most of us are not patient enough to work hard in order to obtain our own nice material things. Even when we do work hard to obtain the better things in life, it all comes too slow for an already impatient generation.

The roots of our obsession with materialism can be traced back to our childhood. A child is an emotional being and it hurts to be taunted by your peers because you are less fortunate. Most of our parents taught us not to worry about or pay attention to the taunts of our peers. It is easier said by our parents than it is to be done by us. Feelings can rule a young person's world and because most young people do not know how to control or vent their feelings, this is exactly what takes place. When a teenager takes the positive route of saving finances or working hard to be able to afford some of the nice things of the latest fashion trend, it seems that the income to get these things never comes fast enough, and all throughout their quest to do better it seems that their peers mock them even harder. Not knowing how to deal with peer pressure leads young people to sometimes do almost anything to get nice material possessions. Most jobs today do not pay enough for a teenager to be able to afford to keep up with the latest designer fashion trends. It can get very frustrating for a person who is working hard in order to be able to buy nice things, but their paycheck prevents them from being able to afford it. Material things are flashed before our eye's day and night. The standard judgment in today's world is to judge people for what they have and not for who they are. Meaning that, what someone has determines who they are. Materialism is so embedded in the culture of this generation that it determines a person's worth. Being in the circle of the popular crowds, having the cutest companions, getting attention, being someone who is noticed as important in the eyes of others depends on the nice material possessions that a person has. This is the way of the world today. Every child, teenager, and adult want to have nice things. Furthermore, everybody wants to feel like they are somebody. Nobody wants to be a nobody. Former generations were much more patient, and they waited until they were older in order to be able to get the nice material possessions that they wanted. However, circumstances sometimes prevent them from being able to get these nicer things when they get older because bills, kids, and other responsibilities hinder them from acquiring these things. Usually as people mature and learn more about life, they learn that the value of life does not lie in how many material possessions that a person may have.

Impatience is one of the main character traits of the present generation. Added to this fact is the constant seduction of materialism that is flashed before the eyes of children today through advertisements, displays, videos, movies, and through the glitter of others. These two combinations create a setting in which quick and easy ways to get finances prevail. In this kind of environment, greed takes precedence over the value of life and people will rob, steal, sell drugs, or engage in any other kind of negative activity in order to excel in this materialistic jungle.

Our minds are so occupied with acquiring the finer things in life that we put more value on "things" than any other aspect of our lives. Why is this? Why is it that this sort of mentality takes root in the minds of this generation more than it has in any other generation throughout the world's history? There are many answers to this question, which in turn tell the truth of this generation's obsession with materialism.

All around us, all we see is the promotion of material things. The people who have the best things are the most recognized and important people. Money makes the world go 'round, but we waste so much money every day. Having the best things is what makes so many of us happy. So much so that we neglect many other more important aspects of our lives. We forget about our physical health as well as our spiritual well-being. As long as we look good on the surface, we are satisfied. But how long do these material things last? Usually they do not last very long at all. We keep these things until they get old or until a new style comes out. Most young people in their recklessness have a hard time taking care of things and making them last.

We actually feel as though material things will make us better people. "Things" are so important to us because we put our value in things. The more "things" that we have, the better we feel about ourselves. Again, this goes back to our lack of morals and the subliminal seduction of the media. If we had the proper moral upbringing, then we would know that our true worth is not determined by what material possessions we may have. The media gives us this image of glitter and glamour as being the best standards in life. Through the movies, magazines, and other advertisement venues, the media subliminally seduces young people into glorifying and worshipping material things.

"Things" are so important to this generation that they are placed above the consideration of people's feelings. People are constantly mocked and scorned because of the lack of materials that they have in their possession. On the reverse end of this, the people who have the best of material items are made to feel superior over other people. Those that have the least of things are made to feel useless and unimportant. So being part of a culture that makes you feel important and worthwhile based on what you have instinctively instills in most people a very high respect for material possessions. This is where the obsession with materialism begins.

If a person is made to feel worthless because they have the least of material things, then it would only seem logical for that person to seek better material things. This can easily lead to an obsession. An obsession is exactly what it has become with this generation. A person whose life is made to feel worthless because they do not have certain things will lead that person to put "things" above everything else in their life. If their life feels valueless without certain material possessions, then they will try to acquire these material things in any way that they can in order to put some value and worth to their lives.

It has been said that young people have come to value material things more than they value human life. As I stated above: "people who feel like their life is nothing without material things will seek these things so that their life is made to feel valuable to them." As long as they remain without these things, life may feel worthless to them, so young people begin to value these things more than life itself because they feel it is these nice material things which give value to life, and when you do not have these things, life in general and your life in particular, is not worth anything. As for those youth who were raised being taught that their worth is not determined by material possessions, they too still become brainwashed with the opinion that their worth depends on the things that they have. Such misfortune occurs because of the youth culture that they grow up in. This type of thinking prevails all over the world. With constant peer pressure and subliminal seduction, it is hard for many youths to apply what they have been taught concerning their real worth versus that of material possessions.

Where does this sort of mentality come from? This mentality is embedded in the minds of this generation. We grew up with this notion. We picked it up from the media and society. Our culture is groomed by the media. Among youth, competition has always been based on who is the best and who has the best things. As far back as people can remember, this has been an obsession among the youth. The phenomenon of the present is the extreme degree in which materialistic obsession has a hold over the lives of most people. Obviously, materialism has become such of an obsession with young people today because of their unlimited access to the media and the corruption of world society. By way of the television screen, magazine pages, and advertisements, today's youth are continuously bombarded with images of glamorous lifestyles. Kids begin to aspire towards this lifestyle, and they try to emulate it as best as they can. In time, it becomes an obsession that they live and die for. The world's people obsession with materialism has reached a very high peak in the present generation. Understanding our culture and digging to its roots clearly allows a person to discover the origin of this generation's obsession with materialism.

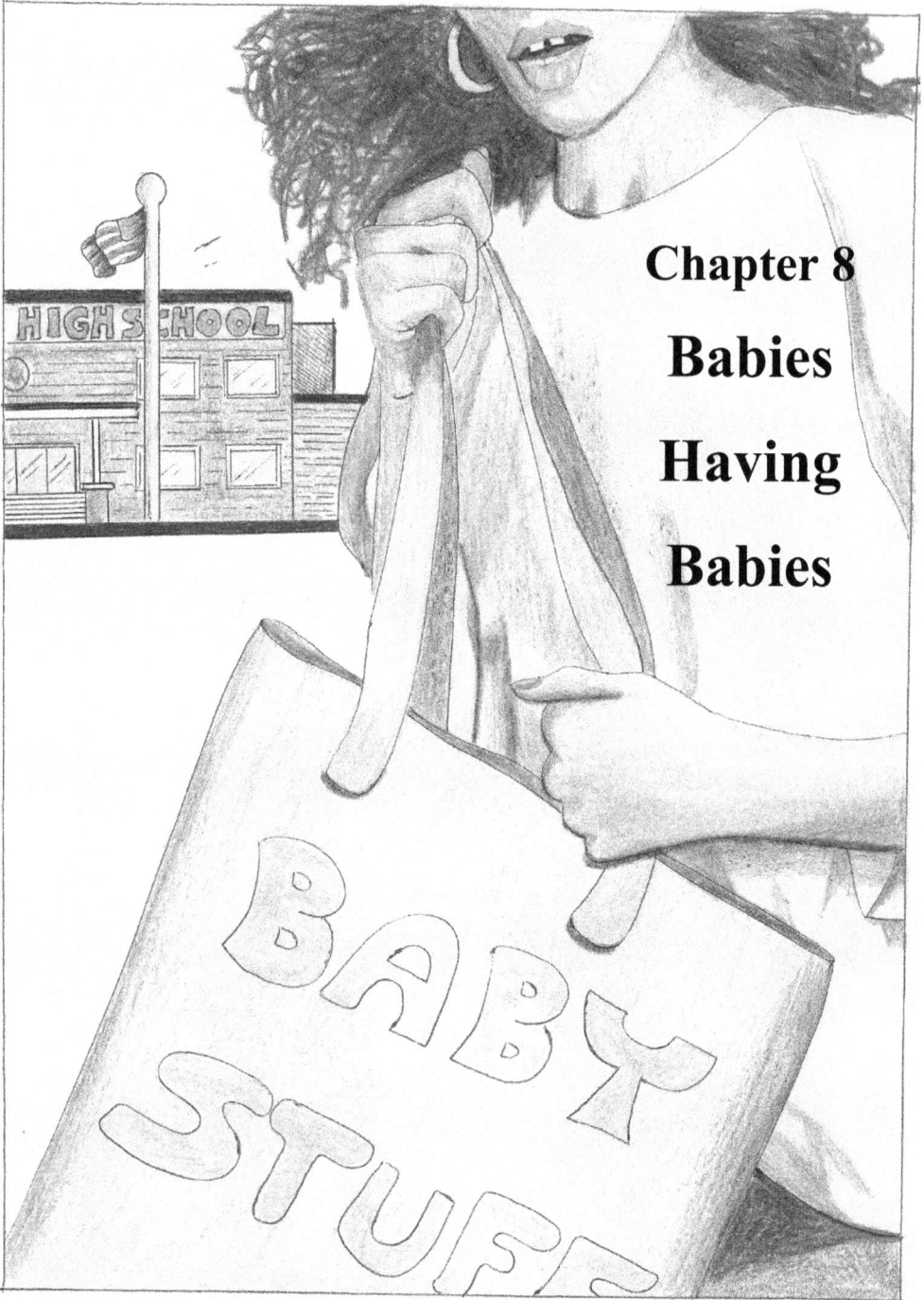

Chapter 8

Babies

Having

Babies

Chapter 8
Babies Having Babies

There are things that developing girls need to know about growing into womanhood. Although they need to know these things, the women around them are not always available to teach them. Many families today are troubled and dysfunctional. The women in these young girls' lives may be at work, fussing at them, or not paying them any attention. Others are giving company to their boyfriends or may be out partying. Some women feel that young girls are still too young to be told about these things. For whatever reasons the women may feel uncomfortable talking to the girl about these things, they fail to realize that young girls need to be told and taught about growing into womanhood. Young girls need to be trained by a woman. They need to be taught how to take care of and manage their womaness as it grows within and outside of them.

Girls have to be taught self-respect, dignity, and self-honor. As they mature into puberty, they need to be told about menstruation and what it is and represents. They need to understand what will happen to their bodies when certain developments take place. Some women somehow think that little girls will somehow learn about these things at school or from another adult woman. But unfortunately, they do not learn the art of becoming a woman through none of these sources.

They often learn by experience. These experiences shape the women these young girls grow to be.

Usually these experiences are not so good. Sometimes they leave the girl confused, traumatized, and misused. The case is even worse when this young girl feels that she was not properly loved in her childhood. When a person needs to be loved, they will seek this needed love through whatever source it may come from. They learn the hard way about true love. But before they learn, they go through tremendous pain at the hands of scandalous men and unsympathetic women. These women who are supposed to teach these girls about staying away from these kinds of men and hormone driven boys do it in such a way that it makes the girls even more curious about sex.

Why? Because many of these women have done the opposite of what they were told not to do when they were girls. Women had trained them before, but they still did the things that they were warned against. So here they are talking to a girl whom they already consider fast for her age, so they already subconsciously think that the young girl will do what she is being told not to do. So instead of teaching these girls in a way that will keep them away from sex, they teach them in a way that makes them curious to experiment in the things that they were being warned against.

Before I go into more details about this, let us first look at the modern culture of this generation. Young girls grow up very fast these days. The sad thing about it is that their mothers and other women around them encourage them along the way not understanding that they are molding this little girl to be a woman. It is not strange at all in this generation to see a 3-year-old girl standing in front of the television watching music videos, doing some provocative dance, imitating the women in the videos. Worst of all is that the mothers and aunties will sit there encouraging the little girl chanting such slogans as, "you go girl;" "Look at her shake herself;" "Don't she look cute girl;" "little so and so is going to grow up to be a heartbreaker."

Everyday in society we see these activities. What is worse is the fact that now days these little girls are even allowed to dress like the women they see in these music videos. They are being allowed to dress and groom themselves like their favorite female entertainers. Most of these female entertainers are labeled as "sex symbols." So, in essence, these little girls are being molded after sex symbols. Many of their young mothers are still considered to be children themselves. They do not even realize, or they are not concerned with the fact that they are breeding a young girl to become an unwed young teenage mother like themselves. These young mothers always say they want more out of life for their daughters, but their actions are always contrary to this intention.

In this generation you will see two and three-year-old girls dressed similar to their mothers. The clothing manufactures profit from this indecent and immoral upbringing of these young girls. Clothing stores are selling skimpy halter tops for toddler girls, etc. Young women of this generation usually buy their daughters these types of clothing because they see nothing wrong with it. In fact, it is the "in" thing. It is considered fashionable and cute for them to dress their young daughters this way.

What these young women do not realize or take time out to think about is what they are doing to the mentality of these young girls. They are teaching them that lewd dressing is just the way of ordinary life. They are sending the message to these young women that it is okay to have men making sly remarks at them in regard to their clothing. Such things are taught by way of example to these young girls. So, in essence, they are taught that they should grow up to be like female role models, who just so happen to be the modern-day sex symbols.

The female sex symbols of today are very different from female sex symbols in the past. The female sex symbols of the past were relatively innocent. In the past, female sex symbols had class, dignity, and respect for themselves. She was intelligent and smart. This is why she was called sexy in the first place. But today, the term of sex symbol takes on an entirely different meaning. The modern-day standards of a woman being sexy depends on how tight her clothes are, how provocative she dresses, and the provocative manner in which she carries herself. Most young women and girls of this generation want to be considered sexy. They think that being sexy is a part of their womanhood.

It is not uncommon to walk in elementary schools and see young girls wearing tight clothing, miniskirts, and heavy make-up. As a matter of fact, if a young girl does not adhere to modern standards, she is marked off as plain and old fashioned. Most of these young girls know every curse word in the book by the age of five.

Girls learn from the women that they grow up around. These women give birth to a girl's conscience. They learn about themselves and what it means to be a woman from the women around them by means of observing how older women carry themselves.

I do not mean to bash. I love my generation, but surely these young teenage unwed mothers are not good examples to teach young girls how to be women. How can they teach these girls what they don't know? In the few cases where some of these women do attempt to teach their daughters to do things the right way, they give a poor personal example by the way in which they carry themselves. Oftentimes these young mothers like to date men, party, smoke, and many other unseemly things. If this is all that these little girls see around them at home and on the streets, then she begins to take on these habits thinking that this must be what womanhood is about. Women make great impressions upon the minds of little girls.

The young girls of today's generation are ahead of their time. They learn very early the things that they should not know. They want to know and experience what the grown women around them talk so much about. Since they are allowed so much time to study and emulate their sex symbol entertainers, they begin to follow in their footsteps. So, in essence, we have young girls who really think that they are women.

Along with their peers, they talk about sex, they see it on television, and they hear about it everywhere they go. Although they have been warned against having sex and messing around with boys, they already have boyfriends with their mother's knowledge. Girls often hear about the supposedly good feeling of sex. So naturally they get curious and want to one day experiment. Nowadays it is sooner than later, and there is always a boy around that is eager to experiment with them.

Usually these girls reach puberty before they begin to experiment. Puberty for most girls begins when they are around ten years old. Womanly features start developing around this age also. Young girls see the women around them showing off their womanly features all of the time, and as a result these young girls imitate these women and start wearing lewd clothing and acting provocative.

Of course, the little boys and men around these girls take notice of them and in particular, their bodies. Little girls love the attention because usually they don't get any attention at home. This makes them do more things to get attention from boys as well as grown men. Therefore, they start to dress even more provocatively. Hormone driven boys are also very curious about sex. When the two sexes get time alone away from their parents, they start experimenting in these things. They imitate the moves that they see adults doing while having sex. Puberty has already set in, but these young girls are not properly told about how they can end up pregnant. Getting pregnant is way easier than they think. An older boy or man comes along, and their experiments turn into a real sexual encounter. The conditions in which this usually happens is not correct at all. Nevertheless, they repeatedly begin to engage in this process. Fresh into their teenage years, these young women become pregnant.

What do their mothers have to say about this? Usually their mothers say such things as, "I knew you would end up pregnant" or "I told your little fast self about messing with those boys," and "I told you that you would end up pregnant because you don't listen." All of the insults do not change the fact that their young daughter is pregnant. The mothers are usually only around the ages of 31 through 36 years old. The daughters often repeat the same process. So how does this young teenage girl learn how to become a mother? Chances are that she will end up becoming a single mother. At first it is hard, but not as difficult as it was for her mother. In today's society, a 15-year-old girl does not live with that much shame because she is amongst many other young unwed pregnant mothers in the world today. These young women can be seen every day freely going on about their business looking very much like they are grown women. Not only do they look like grown women, these young girls also think and act like grown women. They give birth to their daughters who see them doing the same things that their mothers before them did. They grow up too fast and end up having a baby when they themselves are still a baby. So, the cycle continues with so many young girls growing up with a false concept of womanhood. And there you have it: babies having babies.

Chapter 9

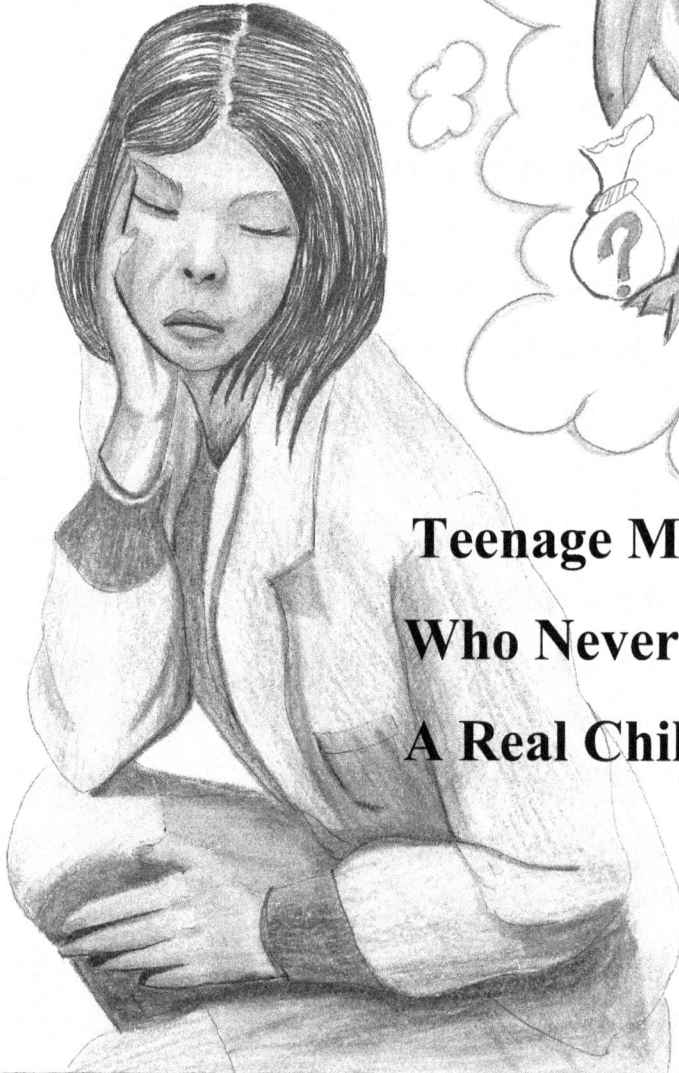

Teenage Mothers
Who Never Know
A Real Childhood

Chapter 9
Teenage Mothers Who Never Know A Real Childhood

A child's personality is formed early on in their lives. Their parents' example as well as their environment, helps to shape the character traits of the child. The reader may look at the name of this chapter and wonder to themselves: "how could a teenage mother never know a childhood?" My reply to this is simply because her parents, her circumstances, and her environment have robbed her of her childhood. She never knew a childhood because she was never allowed to be a child. Her parents reprimanded her and chastised her while she was still a toddler as if they assumed that this little girl knew that every action of hers was wrong. Many young girls of this generation regularly received beatings early in their lives. Communication was done a lot through punishments and chastisements.

Never too familiar with a real childhood, these girls were taught self-survival skills early in their lives. As children and adolescents, they were usually left unattended and alone. They learned very early how to cook, clean, and do for themselves. Young girls take on the role of women by the time they are seven years old. A lot of their parents are out working while they are left home to substitute in their mother's place for their younger siblings. Young girls these days start their menses at nine years old. At this stage they begin to step out of their childhood and into puberty. Circumstances have already prepared them to be women as well as mothers, so by the time they reach puberty and develop womanly physical features, they subconsciously take on the notion that they are grown women.

Parents may warn a young girl to stay away from boys. They may even tell their young daughters that sex is prohibited outside of marriage. Even when they tell them that sex is wrong, they do not tell them why sex is wrong. Furthermore, they do not tell young girls the sacred purpose of sex. Girls are curious. In those instances, where their parents are not their sole teachers, society and the media become their teachers because this is what their time and attention is given to.

Often those mothers that go through emotionally reckless marriages find it hard to teach their children about marital bliss, leaving the door open to promiscuity and unwed sex. Both of these are the sole contributors to teenage pregnancy.

Some teenage mothers have children because they feel empty inside. They want someone to love them with no strings attached. They want someone who will totally need them. When they cannot find this in a man or family member, they assume they can find this in a child because a child will be totally dependent upon them. They figure that a baby can fill this void in their lives. The disappointing thing that they come to find out is that no one can fill this void that only they themselves can fill. The emptiness that they feel is there for most of them because they really never have a chance to experience their childhood. Half of them grew up very fast because they never really felt like anyone was there for them. Therefore, they pretend as if they did not need anyone, and as a result they missed their childhood and took on the mindset of an adult at a very young age. It was in their teenage years that the emptiness from their childhood came back to haunt them. It was then that they recognized that they needed someone. When they reached out to men, family members, and friends, they quickly realized that they were not the ones that could satisfy this craving need that they have had since their childhood. Such an inclination towards this craving to be needed by someone prompted them to have a baby with the thought that having a child would somehow work magic and fill this void in their lives and make them whole.

Contrary to what most of us think, some teenage girls do deliberately get pregnant. These teenagers get pregnant because they want to experience the mother-child relationship that they did not have with their mothers. As they search for love through their child, they finally come to realize that this is not something that they can be in control of.

As long as a baby is being a baby, these teenage mothers know that they have something in which they love that will not hurt them. Even when the father is not around to help raise the child, the single mothers are still encouraged because they are certain that they will be all the parents that the baby may need.

The problem is that these young teenage mothers do not realize that parenting is more difficult that it seems. Many of these teenage mothers did not have a good example in their mother, so parenting turns out to be even more difficult for them. Without a good example these young girls often develop mothers' skills by instinct and through experience as they raise the child.

Looking at the world today, we see many children who are not being allowed to be children. They are being forced to work because of the poor economies of their countries. Young girls are being forced into marriage. In developed countries kids are growing up too fast and missing their childhood. When a child is not allowed to be a child, then that child has no choice but to take on the mindset of an adult in order to survive. Young girls have always been expected to be more mature than boys. Girls have been told to carry themselves like young ladies. At a very early stage in their lives, they are subconsciously taught that girls should behave like women and not like little children. This is the beginning stage of teenage mothers never really getting to know their childhood. As they are indirectly sent the message that they are supposed to be young ladies, they begin to feel older than they really are.

Furthermore, girls develop sooner than boys. All these known scientific facts did not pose a threat to the women of former generations because they were not losing their childhood back then. In their coming of age, childhood was something that was cherished by everyone. The world moves so fast today that childhood only seems like a passing phase in a very short life.

We will add more detail to the answer as to why so many young girls of the present generation do not get a real chance to experience childhood. It is hard for a child to be a child when she is told that she should act like a young woman. Girls want to be girls, but when they play rough or careless like a child does, they are often called tomboys. Girls are told that they should not act like tomboys because it is unladylike. The concept of being feminine is constantly stressed to young girls. The modern concept of femininity includes being sexy. As I pointed out in an earlier chapter, the modern definition of sexy is totally different from what it meant in the past. Sexy nowadays includes a woman who looks erotic and wears suggestive clothing and other notions that do not measure up to the true definition of womanhood. Being taught thus, young girls aspire to be feminine by being sexy. The problem with the present generation of girls is that they are trying to be sexy in all of the wrong ways. When young girls start being feminine under a false illusion of being sexy, they begin to lose their childhood trying to be women when in fact they are still a child.

When girls start dressing and acting like women, they also begin to think like women. Such thinking prevents these girls from thinking like the children that they are. If children are not thinking like children, then they are not truly experiencing their childhood.

In their attempt to be sexy, young girls are being taught all of the wrong things. Therefore, they begin to dress sexy and act sexy. Soon they are approached by men seeking sex. Many young girls accept these advances for various reasons. Fornication is not looked upon as a major sin in the world today. Young unwed couples engage in sexual intercourse on a regular basis. Such unrestricted casual sex is responsible for so many of the teenage pregnancies that happen around the would today. The tragedy that occurs in this is the fact that the majority of these young teenage mothers never really knew a childhood. Growing up too fast has prevented them from experiencing a full childhood.

Chapter 10

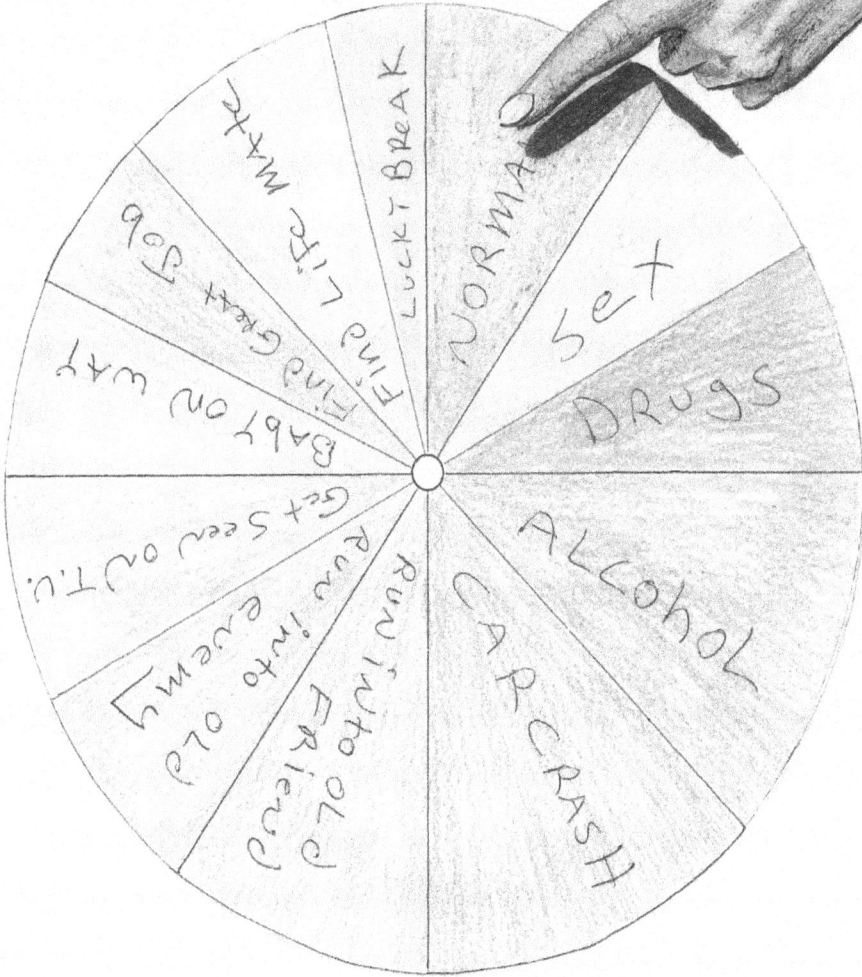

Victims of Circumstance

Chapter 10
Victims of Circumstance

Is there any truth to the saying: that children are only a reflection of their parents? It has often been said that the behavior of a child is a result of their upbringing. Okay, now if the above statements are true, then the direct ancestors of this generation should see the role in which their influence has played a part in the shaping of this generation. This generation does not blame our parents for the way we turned out, but society and older people have heavily influenced us. A child only imitates what it sees around him or her. For the most part, the majority of this generation are still babies, and someone taught us what we know.

We were not born with the negative dispositions that we display in the world today.

There are many people from the older generation that sustain a prejudice for this generation. This hatred can even turn into active bitterness. When older people see us hanging out and engaging in the activities that we do, they look down on us with discontentment. The fact of the matter is that no matter how much the older people disown and look down on us, we are still their children. We come directly from their wombs and loins. So, who taught us what we know? It is true that this generation's actions are ten times worse than that of former generations. There are a number of factors that help shape the present condition of this generation.

It can be logically said that this generation is a victim of circumstance. The reader may ask how can this be? The first cause lies in our upbringing. As children, we were molded by society and older people. Many of our role models are negative. The media and society seem to focus on their lifestyles more than anything else that goes on in their lives.

This generation was born into a drug filled, war torn world. Most of the violence and chaos they have embraced and become known for in their culture was already here in this world before they were born. Certain ills of the world have become signature for this generation because young people have taken things to a new level and have put on a more radical twist in expressing themselves. A generation growing up in a world of problems cannot help solve those problems without the proper guidance. More than anything, they often become a part of the problem. But the question is: are they the problem? This generation was born into the problems the world faces today, therefore they cannot be blamed as being the original cause of any of these problems. So, since this generation was born into this world of problems, we must ask ourselves, is this generation merely a victim of circumstance?

A victim of circumstance is described as one who is put into a situation that they have no control of. Sort of like being in the wrong place at the wrong time. It is a part of life and it is a role that we all play at some point in our lives. But in this case, this victimization has struck at a whole generation.

Born into this world with all of its problems and troubles, this generation can surely be considered as a victim of circumstance. But yet this generation is seen as the offender and not the victim because so many young people only make the problems of the world even worse because of their actions. Another major misunderstanding is caused by the misinterpretation because this generation is not the kind of victim that is looking for sympathy. The children of today and tomorrow have been victimized in the sense that the majority of their problems are not the result of their own making. The problems they are faced with in the world today were already here waiting for them when they got here. Without good examples to show them how to do things in the right way, our children went astray. In this sense, they are the victim because they fell into the trap that was waiting for them.

As was said earlier, children only imitate what they see around them, and the older generation did not set a good example for most children. All of the negative behavior that children display is learned behavior. Whether they learned it through the media or from their elders, they picked their bad habits up from somewhere. Now if these kids learn most of their negativity from the media, should their parents be blamed because of this? In modern times, children are raised and influenced by much more than just their parents. In many households the media and society have a greater influence on children than their own parents do. In fact, many children are the exact opposite of their parents.

Who Is There to Blame For the Way That This Generation Has Turned Out

This is a much-debated question. Who is at fault for the condition of generation next? Is it the media? Is it their parents? Is it society? Is it their elders? Who is there to blame? I guess that you could say all of the above are somewhat at fault for the present condition of the up and coming generation. All of the above sources play a major part in the upbringing of our children. It would be unfair to put all of the blame on one source in particular. In an earlier chapter of this book, it was explained how the media in itself is at fault with all of the negative messages that it sends to our children via its many outlets (e.g., television, radio, internet, magazines, and newspapers). The media is guilty of condemning our children and is even more so guilty in playing a very negative role in the way that generation next has turned out. It is because of the media that our children are exposed to so much sex and violence. The media overall plays the biggest part in influencing most of the negative things surrounding this generation.

One of the most controversial questions asked today is whether or not the parents are responsible for their children's actions. The question is asked if the parents are at fault because of the way their children turned out to be. Of course, a child has a mind of his or her own. A parent can teach a child, but that does not mean that the child will behave in the manner that they were taught by their parents. A child is taught by many different sources. All of these various sources help to shape the adolescent that the child grows into. But this in itself does not absolve the parents from blame. The parents are a child's first teacher. Parents are supposed to teach their child by way of example. The problem is not so much as what parents do not allow their children to do; it is what they do allow them to do. For instance, a parent can be a fault for letting their children watch too much television. Parents should be aware and put some restrictions on their children from watching all of the filth and negativity that is constantly displayed through the media. Taking this into consideration, parents should also put time limits and constrictions on how much television their children watch. If a parent gives their child unlimited access to the television without any guidance or supervision, then that parent is partially responsible for the way that their child turns out. Of course, it will be unfair to place blame on parents if their children sneak and watch television shows that they have been prohibited to watch. If their parents do not have knowledge of what the child is doing, then their parents cannot be blamed for that.

When can parents be blamed? Parents can be blamed if their actions contradict everything that they teach their children. If they do not practice what they preach, then they can produce some rebellious children. Hypocrisy causes children to rebel and that is why you see so many youths who are defiant and rebellious towards their elders. Parents cannot afford to be hypocritical under a child's watchful eye. Such contradictory actions send the wrong message to a child. The same has to be said concerning the elders of children today.

Some elders feel guilty about the way that this generation has turned out because they know that in part it is their fault. They see their children are making the same mistakes in which they made. They see this generation falling into deeper pitfalls and it only deepens their guilt. Other elders are regretful that they did not provide their children with the right amount of love and care.

A mistake is made when parents attempt to prepare their children for the real world by showing their children "hard love." Oftentimes when parents show their children "hard love" it only serves to harden the child's heart. The outcome of this is seen in the violent way that many youths are living their lives today. There is a combination of things that weigh in on how the older generation is shaped, molded, influenced, and is partially responsible for the way this generation has turned out. By virtue of being born into this world, this generation was put in a circumstance and later on became a victim of that circumstance.

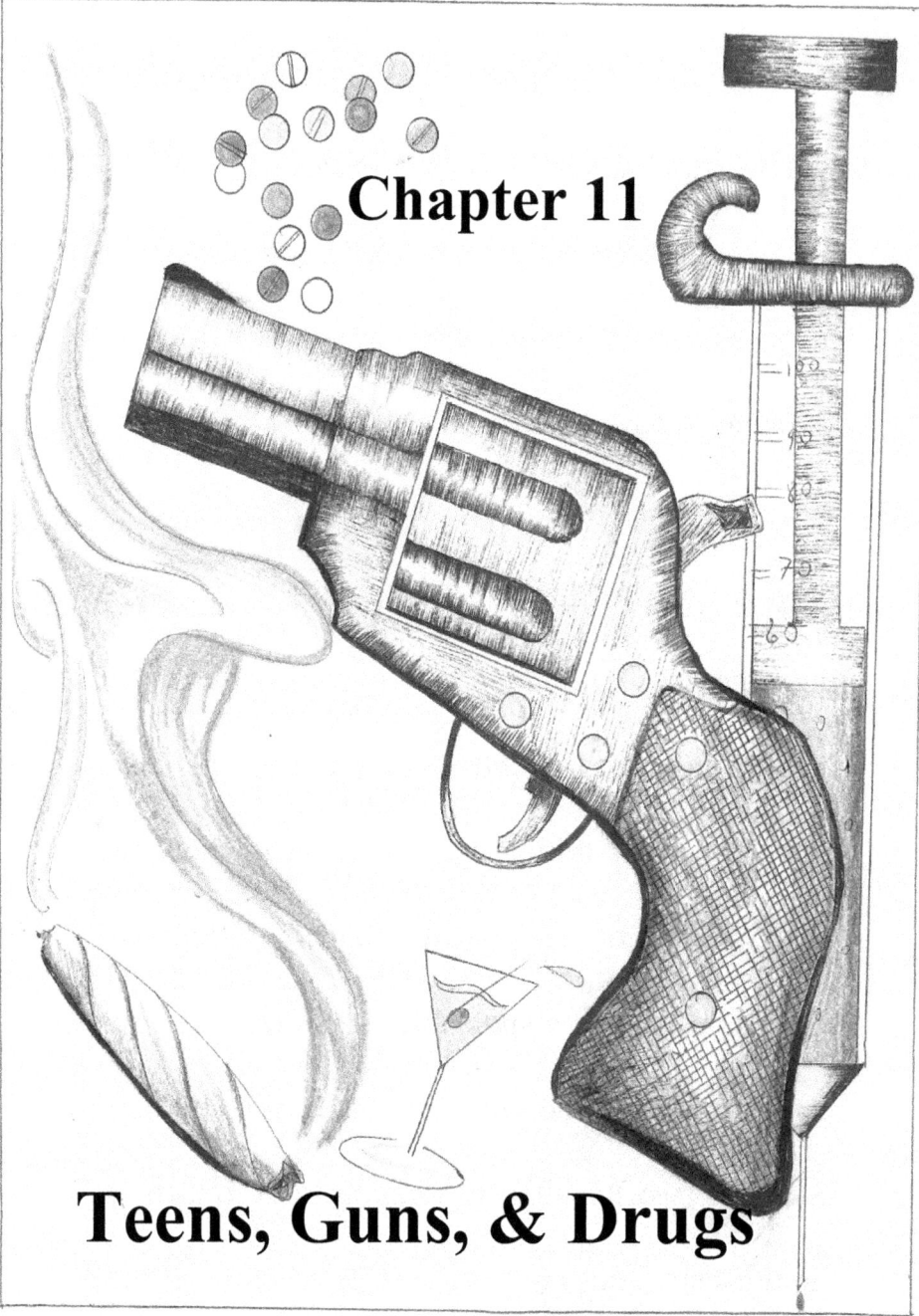

Chapter 11

Teens, Guns, & Drugs

Chapter 11
Teens, Drugs, and Guns

T eens, drugs, and crime are often said in the same sentence. Drugs and crime are two of the main dominating factors of the teen culture. This trend started decades ago but has grown to tremendous proportions. Doing drugs is a regular part of life for many teenagers and they see nothing wrong with it. It's just a daily activity for them. It is a way for them to relive their stress. Teenagers are faced with many pressures and they deal with a lot of stress. A person's teenage years is considered to be the most difficult period of their lives. It is a constant state of transition as a young person searches for their identity. The average teenager does not look upon using drugs as a crime. The laws of society that labels using drugs as a criminal act is rebelled against by many youths.

There is a pattern in all of this that can be linked back to childhood. Many children have already had a controversial misunderstood childhood, and their teenage years only introduce them to even more turbulent times. Children are treated a certain way in modern times, and it is hard for kids to be kids. They are not understood well because nobody really takes time out to understand them. They grow up confused and drugs become the perfect outlet for them to temporarily escape some of the pressures they are dealing with. Drugs become a haven for some youth.

What Substances Do We Define As Drugs

Any unnatural chemical that is taken into the body is considered as a drug. There are good drugs and there are bad drugs. Even those good drugs that are used for medical purposes may be abused and used for the wrong reasons. There is an extended list of the many drugs that are on the market today. We will not go into a detailed discussion about all of the many drugs that are out there today, but we will talk about the most common drugs that are popular among teenagers today. Number one on the list is cigarettes. Cigarettes are considered as a drug because they contain an addictive substance called nicotine.

This is the most common drug used by young people. In fact, cigarettes are legal. By law a person is required to be 21 years of age to purchase and smoke cigarettes every day. Many parents have knowledge their children smoke cigarettes, but they do not do anything to stop this. Most of these parents are not a good example because they smoke cigarettes also. This troubling issue seems to fade further away from being one of society's concerns. People have come to except that kids are going to smoke one way or the other. It is a major problem. Cigarettes are a drug and can cause bad health and ultimately lead to an early death.

Next on the list is alcohol. Kids drink alcohol every day. This is known to be a major problem, but adults are helpless as to finding a solution for this. Young people get liquor from many sources. It is not hard at all for them to get. Alcohol is legal. By law a person is required to be 21 years of age or older in order to purchase alcohol, but like everything else kids have their ways of getting around this. And they consume alcohol in large amounts on a daily basis. The most known tragedy that is associated with this is drunk driving. Many deadly accidents are attributed to kids getting drunk and driving while under the influence of alcohol. Drinking allows young people to unleash their wild side. While under the influence of alcohol, people are known to do some irresponsible things. Adolescents are no exception to this, and in fact they are known to do some of the wildest things after drinking alcohol. Young people start drinking as early as 13 years old. Many of their parents' drink and a lot of our children's problems with drinking has been linked to a birth predisposition to alcohol. Meaning that there could be a medical cause for their early addiction to alcohol. It is said that if a parent is an alcoholic, then their child can be predisposed to drinking through the passing genes from the parent to the child. Alcohol can be addictive, and it is a drug.

Third on the list of the most consumed drugs by teenagers today is marijuana, or commonly known today as chronic or weed. Smoking marijuana is very popular among adolescents. When they smoke it, they are said to feel good. It is relatively cheap, and kids have easy access to it.

The feel-good effect that marijuana gives a person makes them want to smoke it on a regular basis. Young people are known to act in a particular way after they smoke weed. This drug is known for helping people to relieve their stress. After smoking weed, people go into a very mellow state of being. Young people love to zone out and get away from it all. Youth are the number one consumers of marijuana.

Fourth on the list that has become increasingly popular among young people is heroin. Heroin is one of the most addictive drugs on the market today. There has been a recent increase in its use by young people. Heroin is very addictive and deadly. It can be either snorted up the nose or injected into a person's veins. Heroin gets a person very high and it is expensive. Its effects make a person very moody. While high on this drug, people nod off and go into a very dreamy escape that helps them to escape reality. This is very enticing to young people who love to escape their boring and sometimes unbearable reality.

Fifth on the list is cocaine. Cocaine is a white powdery substance that is usually snorted through the nose. It is a very expensive and addictive drug. The effects that it gives a person is that it speeds them up and quickens the senses. Young people get very hyper and active while high from cocaine. Youth consume this drug daily as they stay in the party groove most of the time. Cocaine is very popular among young people.

There is another form of cocaine called crack that is smoked through a pipe. It gets people very high and is very addictive. People who smoke crack will do anything to get it. Prostitution, robbery, and theft take on tremendous proportions as a result of young people trying to support their crack habit. Harsh drug laws have not deterred people from smoking and selling crack.

Speed is sixth on the list. Speed is both heroin and cocaine mixed together. Its high is just a combination of the two drugs as one. It is said to put people in a delusional state.

Virtually there is an inexhaustible list of drugs that are popular and consumed by young people. Here we only wanted to give a brief overview of the most common drugs that are being consumed by young people. There are countless other drugs out there and a new drug hits the market on a regular basis. A brief list of the other drugs that young people frequently take are acid, LCD, PCP, volumes, uppers and downers, syrup, paint, glue, mushrooms, meth, angel dust, and a pill called ecstasy. Ecstasy has grown ever more popular. It is commonly known as "X" and can be disguised in many fashions. Kids have been known to do this drug while sitting in their classrooms. This is because it can be camouflaged as candy. It is very cheap and stimulating. Many dangers are associated with this drug. This particular drug is called ecstasy because it supposedly makes a person feel like they are in a state of ecstasy when they take the drug. So, as we can see there are many drugs that young people are taking. Nearly all of them are addictive and even those legal drugs like alcohol and nicotine are being used daily by our children.

The world is stockpiled with drugs, and our kids have no problem finding drugs. Politicians want to eradicate drugs from society, but more importantly they should focus on eradicating the need for people to want to take the drugs in the first place. We so often deal with the symptom and not the cause. If not drugs, then we would be faced with another dilemma. So, what we really need to deal with is why do our kids do drugs in the first place. We cannot blame this on peer pressure alone because most youth do drugs on their own free will influenced by their need to find a way of release. It is also true that the media plays a major part in influencing our children to use drugs.

Getting high is such a cool thing among teenagers. Most of them see it as harmless. Parents warn their children about taking drugs, but this warning is usually not strong enough to deter their kids from using drugs later on down the line. Why do drugs have such a strong appeal to our children? Almost anything that can help our kids escape what they consider as a boring reality appeal to them. In this sense, drugs and the media mix. Our children are heavily influenced by both of these sources. In the media, drugs are portrayed as cool and hip. On screen and off screen, most of our children's favorite entertainers and actors use drugs. There are also numerous other sources from which our children are influenced to use drugs.

Why Do Our Children Choose Drugs
To Escape Their Pressures

There are many positive things that people can do to relieve themselves of their stress. So why do our children choose to use drugs to do so? Drugs are the easy way out. These chemicals alter your mind and put you in an illusional state of peace. Teenagers are always trying to escape the world whether it be through television, daydreaming, using their imagination, or doing drugs. Since drugs have a real-life effect, teenagers are very quick to take them. Drugs are everywhere and young people have easy access to them. This sort of action goes on around them all of the time and is very easy for them to get mixed up in. Our children are faced with drugs from every direction and some of them easily succumb to the pressure.

What do drugs have to offer young people that other sectors of society do not? Society only seems to present more confusion and controversy to our children. On the other hand, drugs offer them an escape from all of this. When they are high, they are feeling good and not so worried about their problems. What problems? Teenagers have many problems and they are dealing with a lot of issues. Adults can somewhat relate to this because they were teenagers. Even those adults that somewhat have an idea of this still cannot fully comprehend the things that go on in the inner and outer lives of teenagers today. Kids face more troubles than their parents did a few decades ago.

Youth do drugs for reasons such as having fun, and to numb the inner pain they are feeling inside. It usually begins with experimentation and easily turns into an addiction. The various reasons why kids are using drugs today have been stated. Overall, we can see why, and we gain an understanding as to why drugs are a major part of the teen culture.

Teens Relationship With Crime

Teens are frequently involved in crime. The relationship of teenagers with crime is such that the two words are often spoken in the same sentence. Teenagers involvement in crime has become an epidemic that plagues the world. More and more young people are getting involved in serious crime. Here we will discuss how teenager relationships with crime begin. The relationship starts for different reasons for most teens, but at the origin of it, there are some similarities. Kids usually start of dabbling in petty crimes such as theft, curfew violations, and other minor delinquent activities. This is true for teens all across the economic sector. Crime for most kids began in their rebellion against society. In an earlier chapter we spoke of this being a rebellious generation. Misguided young people do not know how to protest properly without committing crime. To escape what they consider as "the prison of their own home" kids runaway from home.

Running away from home is considered a crime in the eyes of the law. When kids hang out on the streets past a certain time, they are violating curfew laws. Curfew violations are one of the more frequent crimes committed by kids. They can be booked at the police station for this and their parents have to come and pick them up before they can be released.

The second most frequent crime committed by young children of all ages is loitering. This is when kids hang out on the corner or on someone's private property. Kids are known for loitering around these places as well as other frequent hang outs. Sometimes people call the police about these kids hanging out, but most of the time, loitering goes unreported because the police appear to be unable to stop it. Even so, there are still many arrests for this crime.

The third most frequent crime that is committed by youth is theft. Our youth do steal quite often and for many reasons. Some of them steal things for the thrill of it. Furthermore, they steal as a symbol of their rebellion against society and the establishment. Kids start off stealing minor things such as gum, toys, candy, video games, etc. Then later, they graduate to stealing things such as jewelry, clothes, and bicycles.

Today's youth desire to be independent and they will steal in order to feel that sense of independence. No one necessarily has to teach these kids how to steal because they will learn how to do it on their own. Some kids do not even know why they steal. They just do it because they can get away with it. I believe that these sort of reasons for stealing are tied into a child's need to rebel.

Unfortunately, there are kids who steal because of necessity. Poor kids who are hungry will steal in order to get a meal. There is a saying that goes, "Some children's only crime is being poor." No one is saying that these kids are justified in stealing. Unable to afford most things, these desperate kids steal for what they need. Half of the time they are caught and given warning. If they are caught stealing afterwards, they may be arrested and sent to a juvenile detention facility. Like most crimes, much of this petty stealing goes unreported.

Also, in our children's rebellion against society, they commit vandalism. This is another crime that is often committed by youth offenders. Vandalism is described as destroying someone's property. Many children destroy things because they are angry. Others do because of a lack of respect. There is another group of youth who commit vandalism because they want the attention that they are not afforded. If they are not seeking attention, why else would so many young people spray paint their names or neighborhood sect on someone's house, store, or shopping mall. If young people cannot achieve international or national stardom, they will settle for the lesser status of a local neighborhood celebrity. In their competitive zones of neighborhood sects, it sometimes takes deadly violence to keep, uphold, and protect this local celebrity status.

This crown is replaced by one person and given to the next as the former is killed or placed in jail. We just talked about stealing among youth, but we did not talk about car theft which is another favorite past time of youth. Why do youth steal cars? The number one reason given is joyriding. Cars make teenagers feel important and they love them. A car is a sign of status for a teenager. For those who cannot afford one or are not patient enough to work hard for one will resort to stealing a car. When they steal cars, they ride around town and get a high from joyriding. They like to be seen and noticed among their peers. Car theft is another major crime that is committed by youth today.

Many of the crimes that are committed by youth today is connected to their rebellion against the world. Drugs and crime are a core part of the teen culture of today.

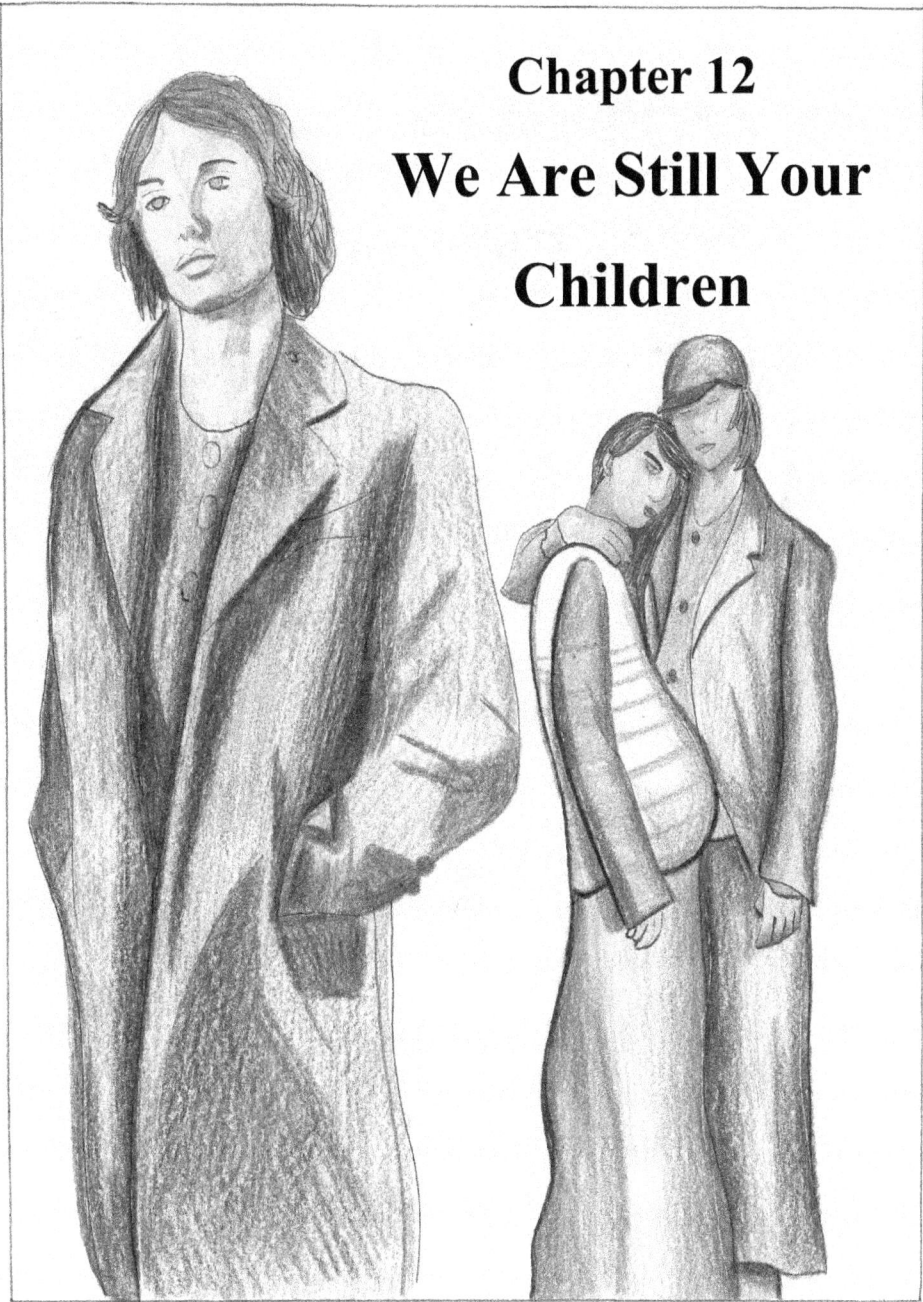

Chapter 12

We Are Still Your

Children

Chapter 12
We Are Still Your Children

No matter how much society and the older generation may dislike the actions and doings of the younger generation, we are still their children. Many older people try to disown the younger generation as if we didn't come directly from them. I know that this generation is violent and even may seem uncaring, but this generation does have a heart that feels. Regardless of how young people misbehave and act wild, parents must realize that even though they did not learn this behavior from them, they still learned it from somewhere. So instead of disowning their children, parents should be trying to reclaim their children. As a result of their different cultures and lifestyles, it is difficult for children and their parents to understand each other.

Although a parent and their children reside in the same household, they often live in two different worlds. A parent's reality is very different from a child's reality. They see life through opposite eyes although they were only born a few decades apart. In this fast-paced world, children grow up really fast; faster than their parents did. Today's children are more aggressive than ever. Many adults despise the fact that children do not adhere to normal traditions.

Many adults are very biased towards youth culture. Young people wearing funny hairstyles, bright colored clothing, nose and lip piercings, tattoos, and other such styles really baffles most adults. In addition to this, when children act so violent and angry today, it causes some of their elders to look upon them in fear.

History has never produced a young generation as cold and violent as this one. When kids are influenced by so many things outside of home, they become more and more the opposite of what their parents raised them to be. Many parents are at a loss trying to figure out what is happening to their children. So much has changed, but that still does not explain why our children have become so disrespectful and violent. Parents fail to see how outside forces can have a bigger influence on their children's lives. The things that kids learn outside of their home and through the media is shaping the people that our kids are becoming today.

In recent times, parents and their children have been growing farther and farther apart. The lifestyles of today's youth have become more radical and extreme. As kids grow older, they seem to become wilder and more rebellious. For some parents, this causes some shame. It hurts these parents that their children are acting out and getting mixed up in all kinds of trouble. It bothers these parents that they did their best raising their children and taught them the correct values in life, and then their own children turn around and defy all that they were taught. It becomes increasingly painful for some parents to see their child in a state of rebellion. Other parents are extremely embarrassed by their children's actions. Unable to deal with this shame, some parents just outright disown their children.

The Rejection of This Generation

The present generation has been rejected from many different angles. Most notably is the rejection that comes from parents, elders, and society in general. Mainly this is due to misunderstanding and a lack of communication between youth and other sectors of society. If adults really understood the root reasons why children rebel, then they would begin to understand their children. Youth and older people stereotype one another so much that it makes it difficult to establish lines of communications between the two parties. Such failure to communicate only widens the generation gap. Many older people simply reject this generation because of their suspicions of young people. Young people are rejected because of their styles, postures, and demeanors.

All the way down to their language; the slang language that youth so often use causes older people to be suspicious of them. Young people are not free of blame because they often do not even try to communicate with older people because they feel like they will not be understood anyway. This only causes more misunderstanding. The nonverbal actions of youth are looked upon as hostile. When youth rebel against society in an unethical way, they are doomed to be rejected. Society, their parents, and their elders should not reject youth simply because of their different lifestyles and cultures. Of course, generation next is going to be different because with time everything changes. In today's world, things are changing for the worst and so are our children. But we cannot forget that these children are the future and we must help them create a better future for the world. If we seek to understand why our children are so angry and rebellious, then we could come up with the solutions to redress their grievances. If we looked deeper into the interior of our children's heart and souls, then we would not fear them because we would have a better understanding of their state of being. If we open our eyes, then we would be able to see the goodness that is inside of our children. We just have to help bring it out of them. The only way we can do this is if we understand that in their present state, our youth are misguided, wounded, hurt, lost, confused, and desperately in need of our help. But they can also teach us a thing or two. Our children are very intelligent; we just need to listen to them. We must see our children for the beautiful human beings that they are. Although they may act wild and crazy, they are still a part of us. We need to take more time out to understand our children and that we would love, embrace, and cherish them instead of rejecting them. Because regardless of what your children do and how they do it, they are still your children.

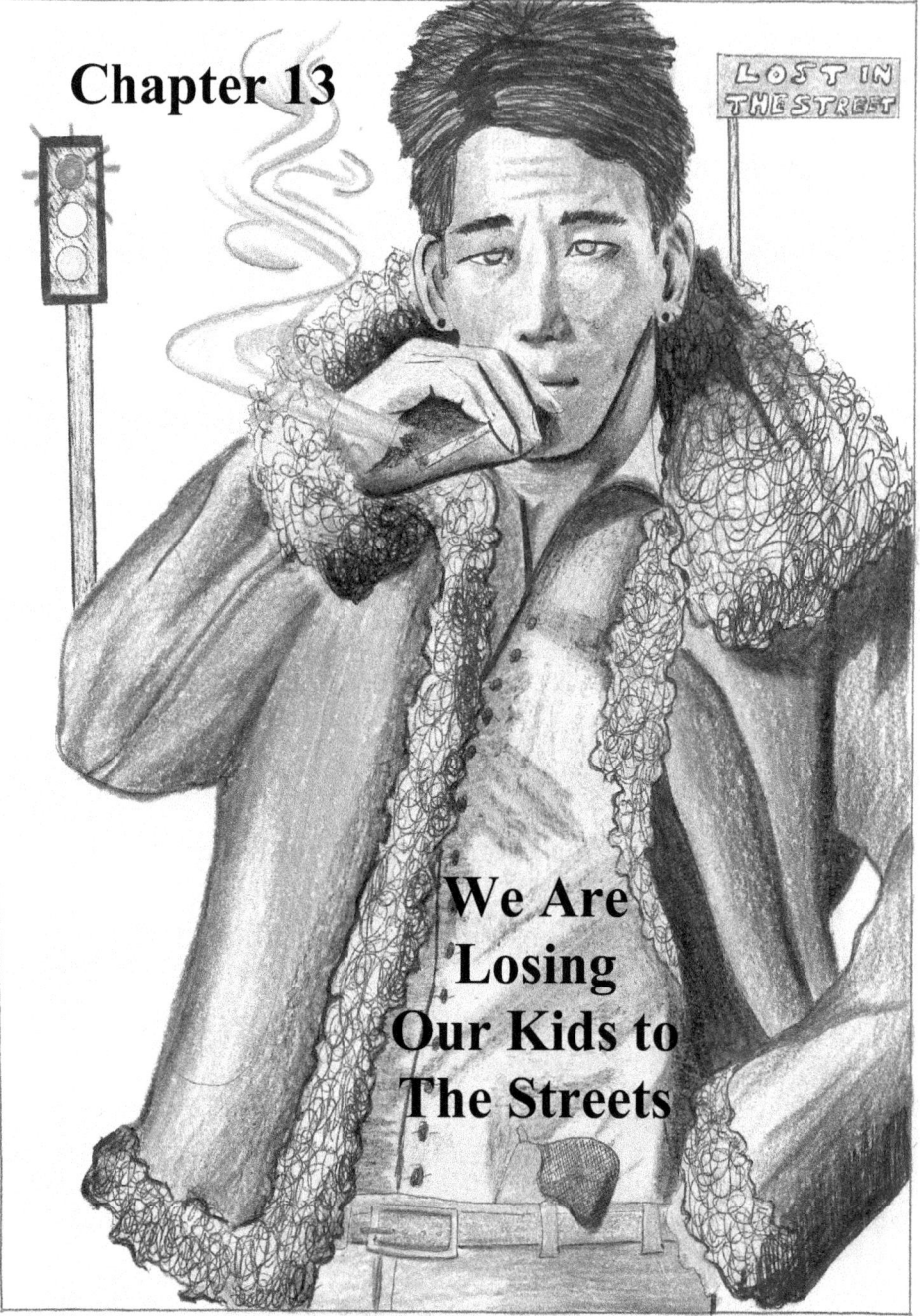

Chapter 13

LOST IN THE STREET

We Are
Losing
Our Kids to
The Streets

Chapter 13
We Are Losing Our Kids
To The Streets

Young people live a life at home, but there is another life that they live on the streets. Home is considered to be safe and the streets are considered to be dangerous. Children and adolescents have to deal with their peers as well as other dilemmas on the streets. When youth are on the street, they are unsupervised. They are faced with many things, and outside of home anything goes. This is what poses the greatest threat to this generation as well as society. Peer pressure challenges youth to graduate from one extreme to the next. We see the disastrous and tragic results of this every day. Our young people's biggest influence is the media, and when they are alone and unsupervised it gives them the perfect opportunity to explore and carry out all of the negative things that they see around them. At home, there are certain things that youth do not do, but on the streets, there are no restrictions. Communities are very loose nowadays. In past generations, every parent in the community helped to raise the children, but today's society is violent and unpredictable. People never know what to expect from parents or their children, so neighbors tend to mind their own business. In this kind of atmosphere, kids behave very unseemly away from home. The streets are a part of today's youth.

The things that our children learn on the streets becomes a part of their character and make up. The streets relate to our children. Although the streets can be cold, they still understand our children. The streets are a place that kids can have fun, and kids love having fun more than anything else. Kids also seek refuge in the streets. The spirit of the streets is very identical to the spirit of youth. The streets are alive. Just like the youth of today, the streets have a spirit of rebellion. An observer can vividly see a picture of pain colored on many streets, and this pain mirrors the pain in which our children are feeling.

For most kids today, the streets are a home away from home. Youth spend much of their time on the streets because most of them feel comfortable on the streets. There is room for them to breath on the streets. While on the streets, children are free to be themselves. The more time they spend on the streets, the more connected they feel to the streets. Our kids get sucked farther and farther into what we consider as the jungle. Some kids stay away from home for as long as they can. They simply call it "hanging out." The problem is not so much as them hanging out, but the problem is what they do while they are hanging out. When our kids get into some serious trouble, it usually involves their friends. Whether the competition is negative or positive, kids are always trying to prove themselves.

Much of the violence that takes place among youth is attributed to what we call peer pressure.

At the origin of peer pressure is what youth have learned from the older generation directly, or indirectly through the media. Older peers teach their younger peers and the cycle continues. By way of peer pressure, children are exposed to and experiment in sex, drugs, and crime. There is hardly a limit to the things that go on among young kids today.

The life that kids live on the streets is very interesting to them. As a matter of fact, it becomes the most interesting part of their lives. This is why we are losing so many of our kids to the streets. What do the streets have to offer our children that other sectors of society do not? Let's look at school for instance. Many young people hang out at school as if they are hanging out on the corner.

When adolescents are sitting in the classroom, their minds are out on the streets. The street mentality lives with youth everywhere they go. The street life is so appealing to some youth that this is all that they are concerned with because the streets are their life. Actually, the streets become their first love. This relationship starts off on a simple basis. After finding the streets have a lot in common with the inner part of them, our youth take a strong liking to the streets. The flirting gets heavy and then from there the dating begins. Youth soon become very infatuated and soon fall in love with the streets. The relationship deepens and soon our youth commit themselves to the streets.

The relationship between our children and the streets reminds us of the battered women syndrome. When our children are abused by the streets, they keep running back. It's like they cannot get enough of the streets. No matter how much physical, mental, or emotional abuse our children receive from the streets, they still remain committed to the relationship with the streets. Duly committed, they cannot see beyond that blind love, just like a woman who is constantly abused by her spouse suffers from the battered woman syndrome.

Outside of parents and the media, the streets have a very tight grasp on our children. It is commonly known that a great percentage of the activities carried out by youth on the streets is negative and unproductive. The majority of all crime that happens takes place on the streets. Most of the youth that have been killed were murdered in cold blood on the streets. For reasons that are known as well as those that are unknown, we are losing our kids too the streets.

How Can We Save Our Kids From The Streets

We can first start by showing our kids that they are loved at home. Many kids seek refuge in the streets because they feel that they are unloved and unwanted at home. But on the other hand, they feel like they are loved and understood on the streets. Second, we can save our kids from the streets by trying to relate to them more. We have to identify with or kids so they will not become so quick to identify with the streets. Third, we can start showing our kids that there are more interesting things happening in life besides the things that they see going on in the streets. Fourth, we can provide them with a good example by doing productive things with our lives outside of home as well as spending as much time at home as we possibly can. Fifth, parents can point out, show, and prove to their children the many dangers that are associated with the streets. Last but not least, parents have to establish a loving home environment for their children and do all that they can to make home a better place for their children than the streets are doing.

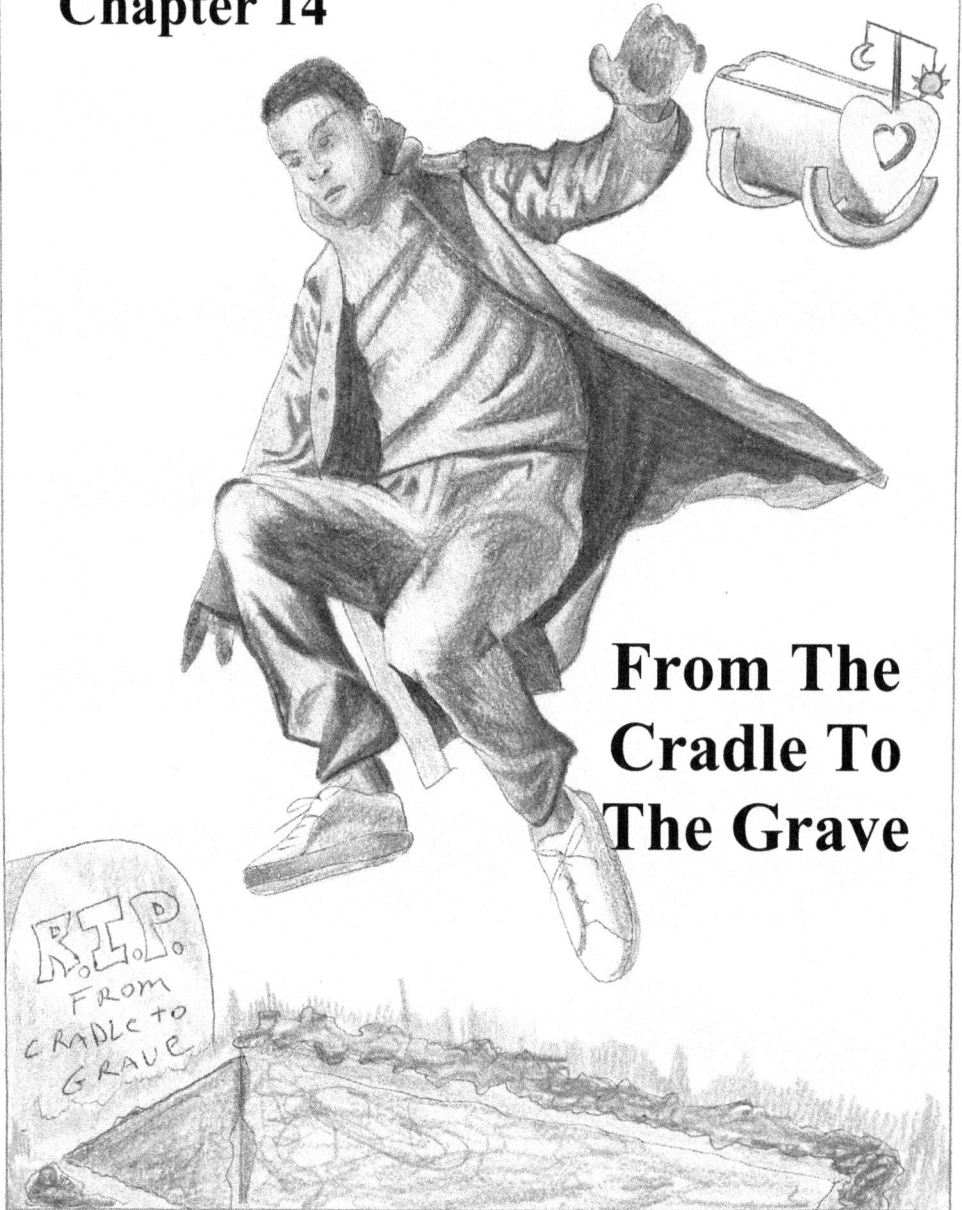

Chapter 14

From The
Cradle To
The Grave

R.I.P.
FROM
CRADLE to
GRAVE

Chapter 14
From The Cradle To The Grave

From the cradle to the grave is a suitable term that fits this generation. So many young people are dying today. Our youth are dying even before they have a chance to live a life. In fact, they are dying so early in their adolescent years that they are going straight from the cradle to the grave. How and why is this happening? If the children are the future, it appears that our future is dying right before our eyes. The staggering number of homicides that are being committed by and perpetrated on youth is astonishing to some, and shocking to others. The first word that comes to people's mind when they hear of this is: gangs. It seems that gangs have sparked this outrageous trend of our youth murdering each other by the millions. Even so, there has to be an origin for all of this killing. There has to be a lack of respect for life for these young people who readily kill at the drop of a hat as well as for those others who put themselves in a position to be killed over some madness.

Where does this lack of respect for life begin? Since life is so sacred and precious, why don't these young people value life? First of all, it goes back to a lack of morals, and second it stems from a sense of hopelessness. When a person is without proper guidance and lost without any real hope, they feel like they do not have nothing to lose. What does life really mean to a person who feels like life has nothing to offer them? Some youth feel that they are at the end of their rope before they reach the age of 18. You ask them why they do not care about some else's life when nobody cares about their life. This is the *me against the world* mentality that so many youths have today. Irrespective of the fact that many youths have caring families at home, these youth feel that their family is on the streets. When they are at home, they feel like strangers. They would rather risk losing their life on the streets than to sit idly by at home and do nothing. Because of their actions they are the black sheep of their families. When their families show disapproval of their actions, these youths feel like their families are rejecting them. This misperceived sense of rejection makes youth feel that they are not loved. Outside of this, they are already struggling with a lot of turmoil as they search for their identity. With these attitudes they hit the streets. On the streets they find other youth who feel the same way that they do. Together they group up and form gangs. Inevitably these gangs take on a negative stance because they are angry, misguided, and misdirected. Without proper direction these youth become involved in crime.

Why Do Our Kids Die For Gangs

We often wonder what is so important about a gang that our very own children would be willing to die for it? What is so appealing about these gangs? First and foremost, we must understand that these gangs are sacred to our children. These gangs are their religion as well as their way of life. That leaves us to ask then who is their God? They pray to the same God that we do, unfortunately they are just lost and misguided. When these kids leave home and hang out on the streets, these gangs are their family. The gang family has more in common with these youths than their biological family does. The gang family accepts the ways and attitudes of these youths. All of these things make them more deeper kindred than the outside world understands. Kids die for their gangs because they live for their gangs. This is their life and their culture, and they will protect it at all cost, even if it means death.

Again, we come to the media and its affects on our children. What does this have to do with death? All day long the media shows people getting killed. From movies to video games there is a constant promotion of murder. All a person has to do is watch the excited response that a child has when he murders his opponent on a video game or sees someone getting murdered in a movie. An observer of this will see how these things can psychologically condition our youth to commit murder. Our kids are not born killers. With so many wars going on in the world, our children are exposed to murder and mayhem. All of this shapes their mentality and the way in which they see the world. Why do our youth murder each other so much? Guns are easily available to our children. With so much mischanneled anger and frustration, our youth lash out at everyone around them, including their peers. What does death mean to a person who already feels that they're walking among the walking dead? For them, death is just something that they walk into every day.

The streets are a jungle, and in the jungle, it is survival of the fittest. Survival in the jungle often calls for killing. Youth kill each other for many different reasons. In the eyes of the rest of the world, these reasons seem very senseless. There are the turf wars and the respect issues. Certain high tempered youth demand respect by all means. Young people today seek respect through violence. They seem to think that violence is all that people understand and that is how they get their point across.

There are two other major causes of death among youth. These two causes are accidents and diseases. Accidental death among youth is usually caused as a result of drunk drinking, drug overdose, and accidental shooting deaths. Youth people often drink and get behind the wheel of a car. Already noted for their carelessness and reckless style of driving, drinking makes this problem even more deadly. When teenagers survive these tragic accidents, they often do not remember their actions leading up to the event. They are usually remorseful afterwards. Their failure to be responsible usually leads to these deadly drunk driving accidents. These teenagers are under the age of 21 so they should not have been in the possession of any alcohol in the first place. But like most other off-limit products, our youth have unlimited access to these things and the results are deadly.

With the arrival of HIV and AIDS, more and more of our youth are falling victim to these deadly viruses. The number one cause of this is unprotected sex. Young people have sex every day. In fact, sex is not even considered as a dirty word anymore. Once again this goes back to a lack of morals. All throughout the media our kids are exposed to lewd sexual acts. Fornication and adultery are promoted around the clock through the media and made to look okay in the eyes of our children. Sex sells and the media exploits this. Their target audience is young people. From commercials to sports, sex is often the theme throughout these shows. Young people are full of sexual curiosity and they reach their puberty at much earlier ages than they used to in the past. Adolescents start having sex as young as 12 years old. Unwed casual sex leads to pregnancy. When this sex is unprotected, it can also lead to deadly disease. Many of the diseases out there are curable. But there is no cure for AIDS. This disease is contracted through a virus tentatively known as HIV. HIV breaks down the immune system making it hard for the body to fight off the disease. Under this condition, catching a common cold can prove deadly. A great number of young people do not go and get regular check-ups and they usually do not find out that they have HIV until it is too late. In the time frame between the time they find out they have contracted the disease; they more than likely have had dozens of unprotected sexual encounters. In doing so, they have passed the virus on too many other young people. Also, these young people whom they have infected have also had sex with dozens of other people and they too have been infected with the disease as well. A child born to a woman with the disease also becomes infected as well and only has a few years to live. AIDS is the number one killer among our youth.

So many kids are dying today. We are losing too many of our children. These are babies that are dying daily. Because that is exactly what they are: babies. Going straight from the cradle to the grave. Not even two decades into their lives and they are dying for senseless reasons. Reasons that are ignorant to us, but for them these reasons are worthy enough for them to risk their lives every day. We do not understand it because we do not understand our children. We think we know but we really do not know. There is much more that we can be doing to prevent our children from going from the cradle to the grave.

Chapter 15

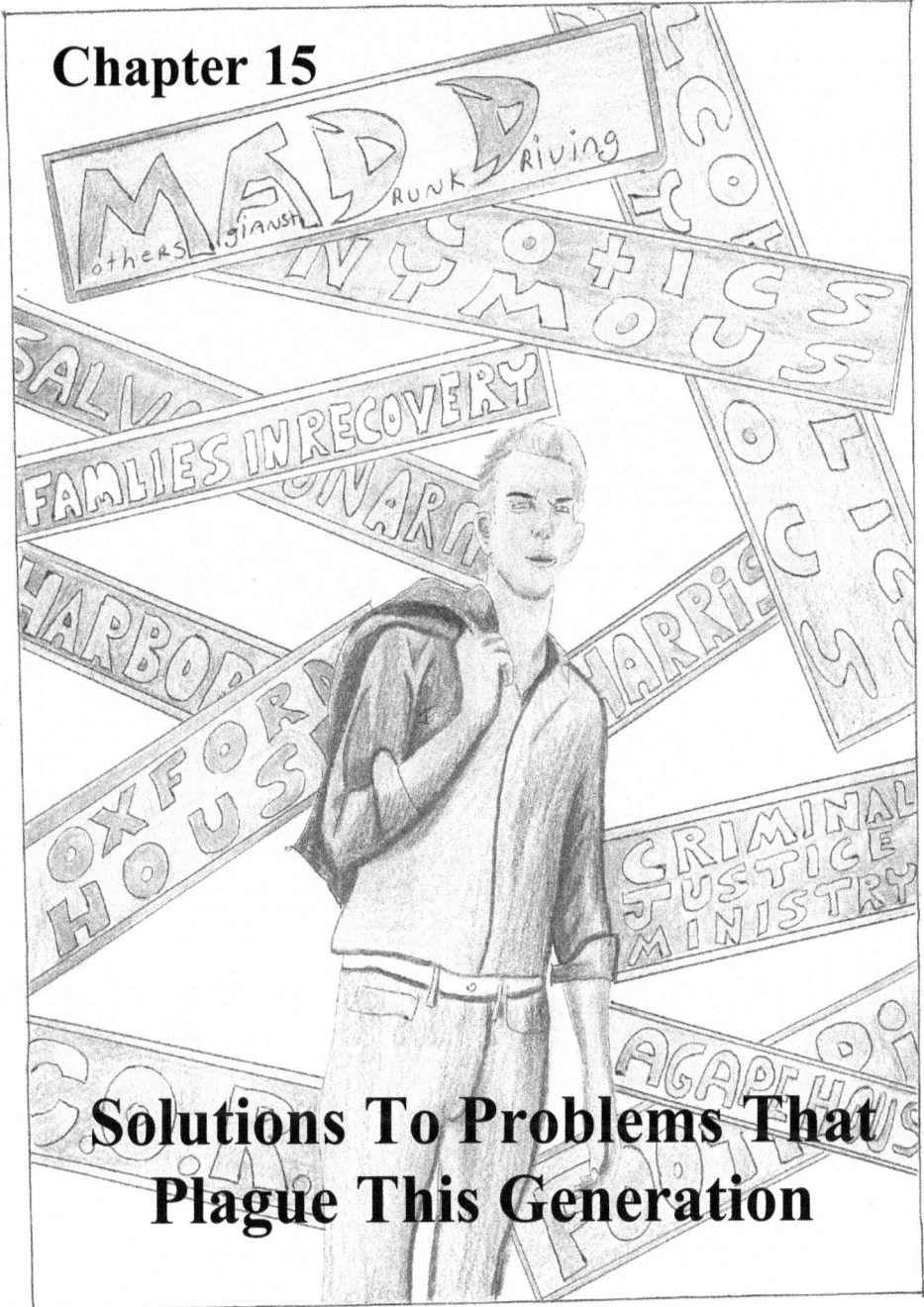

Solutions To Problems That Plague This Generation

Chapter 15
Solutions To The Problems That Plague This Generation

Cycles continue and patterns repeat themselves. So we must ask ourselves; what is "The Solution" to the many problems that plague this generation? If there is more than one solution, then all of these solutions have the same aim and serve the same purpose (i.e. that being to save this generation). So, for clarity, we will dub all of these many solutions simply as "The Solution." And when we come up with a solution, what is the best way for us to approach this solution? Unfortunately, no matter how hard we try, most of us do not know how. There are many solutions, but the question remains; what is the best way in which to approach these solutions as one, and in the best manner in order to come up with the best results?

Disagreements and different approaches to the problems keeps people from mutually coming together and joining forces with their ideas to unite and formulate the ultimate solution. Well ultimately, the best point of view, full of the most creative energy and personal experience with the most at stake comes from those young people of this generation. This generation knows that there are many things about its cultures and ways of life that it needs to change. But before they can do so, they need help and guidance. The final question is: what do we have to offer?

With our children crying out for help and us reaching out to give them help, we should be able to come up with a solution to their problems. We must also realize that their problems are our problems as well. The children are the future and without them we have no future because we will only see the future through our children. Therefore, it is incumbent upon us to come up with a solution, namely "The Solution." Now, where do we start? First, we must reverse the murderous mentality of our children. Because if they are busy killing each other, then they have no time to sit down at the table of negotiations. We first have to deal with the origin of this mentality. Earlier it was stated that our children kill because they have a lack of respect for life, and this is because they feel unloved along with not having been taught the proper morals.

We have to let our children know that they are loved. Better yet, we have to show them that they are loved. This generation does not heed to lip service. As a matter of fact, this generation is so rebellious because it is sick and tired of the hypocritical actions of society. Our children must be taught by better way of example. If we are to reach them, we have to teach them the truth, but most importantly we must live by that truth. Everything starts early in their childhood. The mission starts then. The minds of our children must be shaped towards positive thinking.

Therefore, we must monitor what mental foods our kids are eating. Most notably, we must make the media responsible for what it shows. Kids must be properly monitored. The creators of video games have to stop making the concepts of these games so violent. Education must be made of more interest to our children.

The people who hold the attention of our children must do the right thing with that attention. The movie stars, famous entertainers, musicians, and professional athletes must start living positive public lives. These people are the role models of our children. At one point in their lives almost every child dream of being a movie star. If these dreams are draped in images of violence, our children will subconsciously aspire towards violence. Movie stars must portray a more positive image for our children, on screen as well as off screen. Since our children want to grow up to be just like them, they must be more positive.

Famous entertainers always seize the spotlight. They grasp the undivided attention of our children. Oftentimes, this spotlight is negative. These entertainers have all of the popularity, wealth, and fame that our children wish they had. Their controversial lifestyles can somewhat relate to what young people go through in their inner lives. Our youth imitate these entertainers from their dressing styles down to their use of speech. This all becomes a part of their ever-changing culture. These famous entertainers are trendsetters among young people, and if they would start setting positive trends, it would have a very positive affect on how our kids turn out.

Last but not least, we have the professional athletes, most of whom are very famous. What do sports represent today? Is it all individualism and no teamwork? Without teamwork things cannot get done, but the star of the team always seizes the spotlight. So many of today's superstars' live lives that are very controversial. The media always seems to have a fresh headline of some negative news about the happenings in the lives of these stars. Such limelight catches the attention of our children. It often turns out for the bad because our kids usually miss whatever lesson was to be taught. Instead, they begin to seek the attention that these athletes get, regardless of whether it is positive or negative.

If we could redirect the most influential people and things in our children's lives, from negative to positive, then we could reverse many of the things that have gone astray in the world today. There are many different approaches to the solution, but this should not cause disunity when everyone is striving to reach the same goal. Our differences of opinion are not more important than saving the lives of our children.

We must downgrade violence and teach kids not to embrace it. We have to try and better understand our children. Their anger is raging, and we must somehow dig to the root causes of this anger. Children must not be denied their feelings.

Our focus must be to help them deal with these emotions in a way that is conducive to themselves as well as everyone else. Youth are extremely different and radical, and this is just something about them that we have to accept. When our children are talking, we have to accept the inevitable change that will come as they grow into their adolescent years. When kids begin to rebel, we must not alienate ourselves from them. Such behavior on our part drives our kids to the streets and gangs. Their need for independence must be better understood by us. We must not attempt to smash their independence because such actions will only increase their rebellion. We have to let kids be kids. The level of intelligence is not the same as ours and this has to be taken into consideration when we are dealing with them. We must have patience when dealing with young people. We must not forget that we were young once before also.

There are countless other solutions that form "The Solution" to the many problems that plague this generation. Here we have only pointed out some of the major problems and suggested some solutions to those problems. We will not look at these solutions as being independent of each other because they all aspire to achieve the same goal. Unity must be sought in this process. Our goal is to save the future of the world, i.e. our children. For every problem there is a solution. The devastating condition of the present generation does manifest a drastic problem that needs to be solved. This is a problem that cannot be ignored, and in fact it is a problem that refuses to be ignored. It is a very loud problem and it stays in our ears and blinds our eyesight as we cannot see an end to it. Our children are demanding to be heard. If we can see the problem, then surely, we can see the solution.

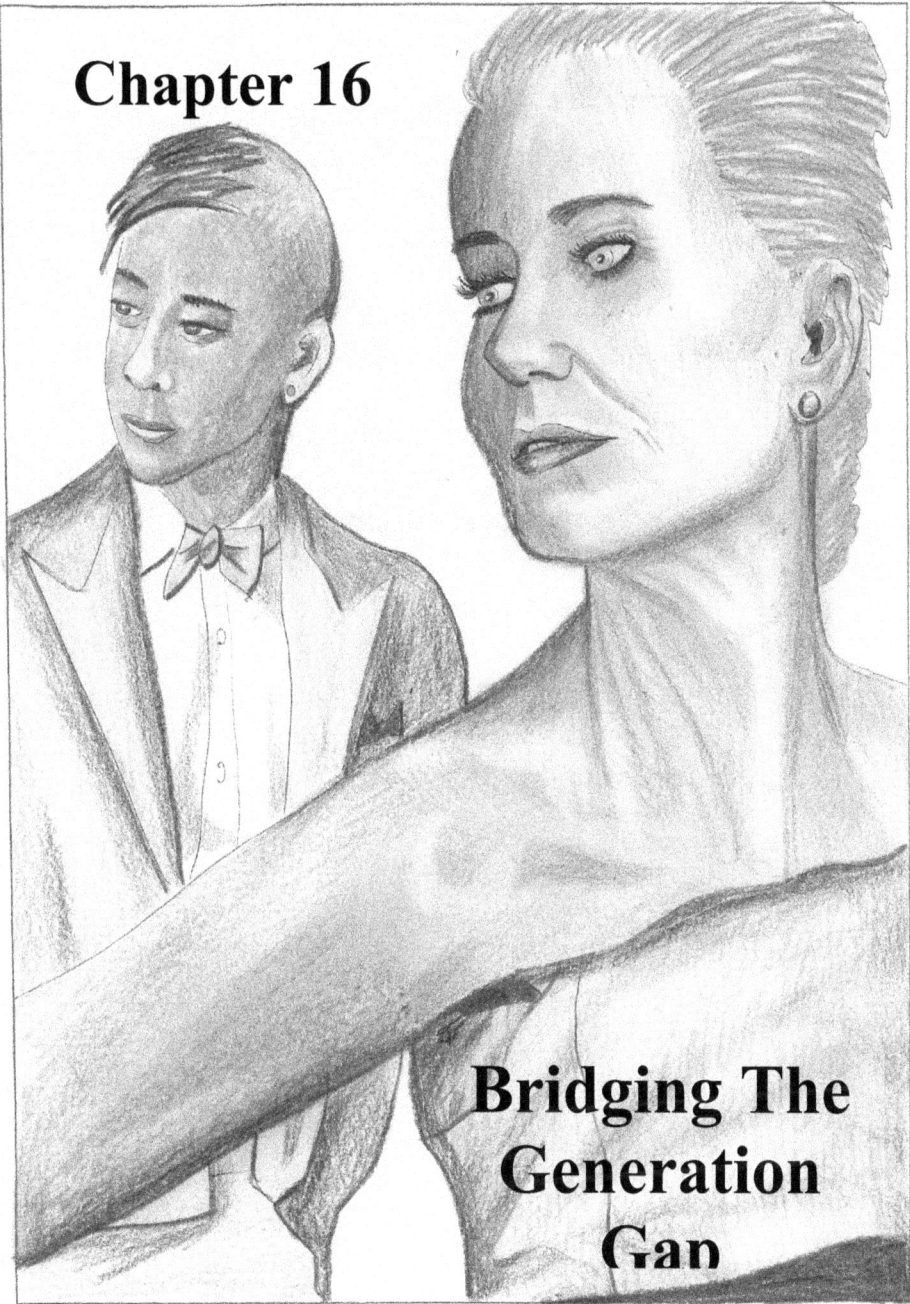

Chapter 16

Bridging The Generation Gap

Chapter 16
Bridging The
Generation Gap

There is a large separation gap between the older generation and generation next. These two generations were only born two or three decades apart, but they have nothing in common. A generation gap is defined as a difference in attitude, or a lack of understanding, between young people and older people. We must bridge the generation gap. In order to do so we must begin to better understand our children and vice versa. Everyone has to meet each other halfway. Never judging a book by its cover is a principle that we must begin to follow. Therefore, we must stop stereo typing one another. United we stand but divided we fall.

Many older people are scared of young people. They fear youth because they have images of them as being violent killers. Parents are sometimes afraid of their own children. The behavior of young people is becoming more menacing each day. The music that they listen to is labeled as "devil music."

This is a very serious problem because it keeps parents and their children divided. There seems to hardly be any reasonable lines of communication between the two age groups. Much of the interaction that goes on is the mandatory communication that has to go on between the two. Misunderstanding begins to turn into active mistrust. Older people are very suspicious of young people. In their eyesight it appears that young people are always up to no good. The fashions, style of music, taste in food, means for entertainment, likes, and dislikes, are all different between the various generations that are still in this world. But in order for us to bridge the generation gap we must focus our attention on similarities and not differences. When we focus so much on differences, we only widen the generation gap.

We can bridge the generation gap. This bridge is not beyond repair. We just have to unite the newer elements with the older elements and make them work together for the benefit of each other. Though the bridge may be different in certain parts, it is still the same bridge. The bridge must be united, because if it is divided, it falls. This is a bridge that all of humanity walks on, so surely, we have to close all of the gaps and make the bridge strong as one.

First of all, people from all generations have many things in common. In fact, they have more in common than the differences that they have. The problem is that the differences are always highlighted and blown out of proportion. This only serves to drive a wider wedge between the generation gap. No matter what generation a person comes from, they are still human. They all need food, water, and oxygen to survive. Each age group is capable of love and seeks comfort in one form or another. We are all members of the human family and we need to come together.

The list of commonalities outnumbers the list of differences. So, this makes one wonder as to why older people and young people so separated? This happens due to the reasons given above, because of the different attitudes and the different outlooks of the two age groups along with the suspicions and stereotyping. If the two age groups constantly focus on their differences, of course the generation gap will only widen. So now we turn our attention towards bridging the generation gap and bringing older and younger people together as one.

How Do We Accomplish This Tremendous Task

Each age group need to better understand each other. Stubbornness must be borne out in this effort. Commonalities have to be highlighted while differences are neutralized. Older people must accept the fact that younger people's culture and way of life is different from theirs. At the same time, young people must respect their elders and their more quite conservative lifestyles. Differences have to be worked out if everyone is to get along. Between the generations there will be differences, and when this is understood in the proper context, it will not be such a problem. The different lifestyles of each group must begin to be appreciated.

Young people need to discard their antisocial attitudes and explain their culture to older people. As long as both generations are stereotyping each other, there can be no understanding. The stereotyping must cease. Only then can the generation gap be bridged.

There are three different generations in this world. We have the generation of grandparents, the parents, and the children. There is also an even older generation. The present generation and generation next are considered as the same generation because the parents are so young when they have their children. So basically, we have various generations still existing on this earth. We have only stressed the older generation and the younger generation because all people who are in their middle ages or older are of the older generation, while everyone who is anywhere below their middle ages or younger are considered to be of the younger generation.

The older generation is patient while the younger generation is always in a hurry. Is one moving too fast or is the other moving too slow? It could be both. Young people do move entirely too fast. As a result, they are losing their childhood and dying too fast. Older people have learned patience from lifetime experiences. Most of them have learned their lesson from living too fast. So now they live their lives slow, but are they living their lives too slow? Life seems to be flying right past the eyes of the older people. It appears they can do more but chose not to. Young people claim that older people do not live their own lives because they are always too busy worrying about what young people are doing. They say that old people are always in their business. This again creates more disunity. Maybe older people are just curious and young people just get agitated at this. Their agitation begins to turn into hostility towards older people and vice versa.

Why Is Each Generation So Judgmental Towards The Other

Maybe if each generation was not so judgmental toward each other, they could come to a mutual understanding. Judgment creates disapproval, and disapproval leads to rejection. This once again goes back to stereotyping. When each group stereotypes the other, they are in essence judging one another. The problem is that they judge each other for all of the wrong reasons. The opinions that they form of each other may very well be wrong. The communication gap is so wide that young people and older people only communicate to the extent that is necessary. The politeness that is usually shown between two age groups is the kind of politeness that is shown when needed, or the kind of fake politeness that is displayed between feuding business partners.

As long as we judge people, we are bound to find some flaws. If we put our attention on these flaws, we soon blow them out of proportion. If it becomes instinctive or either a habit for us to judge people from a different age group, we are bound to begin to form incorrect judgments of them. Then we will call ourselves disliking people whom we have never had a chance to meet. This happens everyday with younger and older people. Stereotyping is a major problem between the two age groups. Young people must make a better attempt to get to know older people and vice versa. This process has to be mutual. The logic in this is that if each age group begins to try and better understand one another before forming a bias opinion, then maybe they can start doing away with their misconceived notions of each other.

Unity has to be reached among all of the parties involved. We have to unify the two age groups so that we can bridge the generation gap. Each generation has a lot of good to offer each other. This has to be realized and acknowledged. Older generations have a lot of knowledge and wisdom to pass on. Young people have a lot of new insight and fresh ideas to bring to the table. Both age groups have to work together for the advancement of human civilization. The children are the future and we all have a responsibility to try and make a better future for the world.

The younger generation can help change the course of the world by seeing the mistakes the older generation has made in government. By bringing their fresh ideas to the table they can run new governments around the world in a more positive way than their fathers before them did. Young people have the potential to change history by not allowing history to repeat itself. In doing all of the things above, the older generation and the younger generation will be uniting and working together for everyone's benefit. By working together, young people and older people will begin to understand each other better. A gap has to be filled with a substance; the substance to fill the gap between two generations is understanding. This understanding has to be far reaching and with this understanding, we can bridge the generation gap.

Other Books by Bobby Bostic

Dear Mama: The Life
and Struggles of a
Single Mother

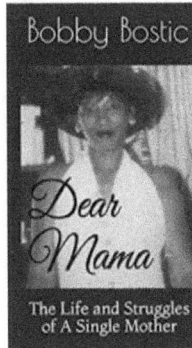

Mind Diamonds:

Shining on Your Mind

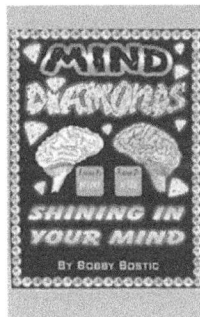

Mental Jewelry:

Wear It on Your Brain

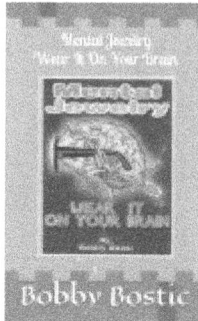

When Life Gives You

lemons:

Make Lemonade

Life Goes on Inside

Prison

Time: Endless Moments

In Prison

Also look for future books, products, and

merchandise by Bobby Bostic.

www.ingramcontent.com/pod-product-compliance
Lightning Source LLC
Chambersburg PA
CBHW081424090426
42740CB00017B/3171